EARLY FLORENTINE
DESIGNERS AND ENGRAVERS

EARLY FLORENTINE
DESIGNERS AND ENGRAVERS

MASO FINIGUERRA   BACCIO BALDINI

ANTONIO POLLAIUOLO   SANDRO BOTTICELLI

FRANCESCO ROSSELLI

A Comparative Analysis of Early Florentine
Nielli, Intarsias, Drawings, and
Copperplate Engravings

JOHN GOLDSMITH PHILLIPS

Published for

The Metropolitan Museum of Art

HARVARD UNIVERSITY PRESS

Cambridge, Massachusetts

1 9 5 5

TO
Giovanna

PREFACE

The present study began simply as an inquiry into the origins of twenty nielloed plaques decorating a silver-gilt cross in The Metropolitan Museum of Art. Soon, however, this problem showed itself to be far from simple. It could not be disassociated from that larger issue of the origins of all Florentine nielli, just as that larger issue could be understood only in connection with the still vaster question of the origins of all early Florentine engraved prints.

These are problems indeed, for the answers to which we have until now been presented with an all but universal blank. The plain facts are that none of the Florentine nielli has ever been securely attributed to anyone, nor are any early Florentine engravings (with the notable exception of Pollaiuolo's Battle of the Naked Men) known by the names of the masters responsible for them. And the dating of both nielli and engraved prints has on the whole been dealt with in a correspondingly indeterminate manner.

This is not to say that scholars of the past are in any sense to be censured for this negative state of affairs; there has in truth been little to go on, and the problems have been far, far more involved than those in the related fields of Italian art. On the other hand, unless we seek refuge in a gospel of defeatism, we must admit that evidence surely exists which if correctly interpreted would lead the student out of this morass of uncertainty. There are, for example, the brief but illuminating accounts of Vasari, Cellini, and others which, together with the few existing documents relating to the matter, have been placed at the beginning of each Section of this study. Then there is testimony of another kind, the stylistic evidence which exists in each and every niello and copperplate engraving. Our approach, therefore, has been a fresh re-examination of these two lines of evidence, the historical and the stylistic. In this we have been sustained by a belief that the problems could and should be solved.

The reader will judge for himself how these efforts have fared, for he will be presented with a theory that will account for much of the early development of the Florentine arts of niello work and copperplate engraving. Whatever the merits of the theory, it should be understood at the outset that there is as yet no final proof for it. On the other hand, the hypothesis would seem to offer a consistent interpretation of a great deal of hitherto unconnected evidence. In actual practice, furthermore, it seems to work. Not, for example, until the many pieces studied in this essay had been assigned to their masters was it possible to answer our very first question as to who made the plaques for the Metropolitan's cross.

Our narrative is divided into four Sections, the first of which is devoted to nielli. The second is a brief study of Florentine intarsia design to the degree that it affects the careers of two of our masters, Finiguerra and Pollaiuolo, and our conclusions regarding their work. The third is an analysis of the drawings in the Florentine Picture-Chronicle, which we discover to be a key for the understanding of the engraved prints. The last and longest Section deals with the many complexities of Florentine copperplate engraving. Our various findings are finally brought together in a brief Conclusion.

There is no point in outlining here the stages of our theme's development. It seems better that it be revealed in a logical manner, as our story itself is told. In this Preface, however, I should like to make two points that may prove useful to those following our account.

The first is that we are dealing with five specific masters, Maso Finiguerra, Antonio Pollaiuolo, Baccio Baldini, Sandro Botticelli, and Francesco Rosselli, all of whom, excepting possibly the last named, are known to have worked as goldsmiths. Regrettably we know too little about Rosselli to enable us definitely to include him among those who had worked in that craft. Such a connection with goldsmithery was natural enough, for it was in the shops of master metalworkers that niello plaques were made for the decoration of a variety of secular and religious objects. In the same shops copper plates were first engraved in the style known as the "fine manner," which was no more than the niellists' technique put to a new use.

We find, therefore, that the tradition closest to the niellist and the early print maker was that of the goldsmith. With the signal exception of Fra Filippo Lippi, whose works will prove to be a prime influence throughout the course of our account, it would seem that questions of style and composition are not to be resolved through any study of contemporary paintings. We clearly see the impact of the Florentine tradition of the metalworker in the productions of such a master as Finiguerra, who was a follower of Ghiberti (himself a goldsmith as well as a sculptor), and whose style was profoundly shaped by that of his master. It is of further interest that we rely on the writings of another goldsmith, Benvenuto Cellini, for a number of our most valuable clues regarding the early histories of the two crafts with which we are concerned.

My second point is that the making of nielli and engravings in Florence was generally a collaborative enterprise. In an examination of any one work we may be confident that we are dealing with the efforts of two men, the designer and the engraver. Now the difference between a design and an engraved version of it is determined by the manner in which the engraver's tool has transferred the drawing to the metal plate. In discussing the designs of the Dutch master Franz Floris, Vasari once commented on such a situation. He wrote: *Vero è che ciò a noi non dimostrano interamente le carte stampate, perciochè chi intaglia, sia quanto vuole valent'uomo, non mai arriva a gran pezza all'opere, ed al disegno e maniera di chi ha disegnato.* (True it is that we cannot see this [his greatness as an artist] too clearly in the prints, for we know that the engraver, even if he were the best of craftsmen, is always far from achieving the effect, the design, and the style of the designer.) Now if this applied to the engraving of the sixteenth century, it was just as true for that of the fifteenth. Hence it is that the Florentine designer's identity was usually concealed, and often cunningly so, beneath a mask that was not of his own making. It is the task of the critic to recognize this mask created by the engraver, and by lifting it to reveal the designer. That this approach has not been followed in the past would seem to go far toward explaining why the early Florentine nielli and prints have so long remained in the limbo of anonymity.

In conclusion it should be stressed that this is neither a history of nielli nor one of engraving. It is no more than a new interpretation of part of the material so admirably brought together by Arthur M. Hind in his single volume *Nielli* (1936), and in the first three volumes of his monumental *Early Italian Engraving* (1938–1948). As definitions for technical terms are to be found in Mr. Hind's text, it hardly seems necessary to repeat all of them. For the convenience of the reader, however, the terms "nielli," "sulphur casts," and "niello prints," which may prove confusing to those not specialists in the field of engraving, are defined on pages xxi f. In the Appendices at the back of the book I have presented a chronological list of the engraved works by Finiguerra, Pollaiuolo, Baldini, and Rosselli that have been specifically mentioned in the text, as well as a list of Finiguerra's works other than engravings mentioned herein.

I gratefully acknowledge that my debt to Mr. Hind is an enormous one. Without the works of this great English scholar as constant guide and reference, the present study could hardly have been begun, much less brought to a conclusion. Mr. Hind's volumes have been a generous invitation to study, and will surely long remain as the foundation for any serious work in the fields of early Italian niello work and copperplate engraving.

I am also indebted to a number of individuals who more than they may imagine have been of help to me. In some instances saving me from committing grave errors, their assistance was all the more valuable since I have been working in fields that are not my own. Among these individuals are Mrs. Werner Abegg, Jean Adhémar, Bernard Berenson, André Blum, Alfred M. Frankfurter, Charles R. Henschel, William M. Ivins, Jr., Richard Krautheimer, Marcello del Piazzo, A. E. Popham, Jakob Rosenberg, Filippo Rossi, Henry C. Rossiter, Paul J. Sachs, Ferdinando Sartini, and

Luisa Sinibaldi. I am especially indebted to Mr. Berenson and Dr. Sinibaldi for their sage counsel, and to Dr. del Piazzo for his assistance in obtaining accurate transcripts of documents in the Archivio di Stato in Florence. A special word of thanks is owing to Dr. Blum, who generously placed at my disposal a number of the photographs used in his recent work *Les Nielles du quattrocento*. Within The Metropolitan Museum of Art, I have had the active encouragement of Francis Henry Taylor, who indeed first suggested that this book should be written, the ever helpful advice of A. Hyatt Mayor, and the generous co-operation of the staff of the Department of Prints. In many ways Olga Raggio has been of constant and invaluable assistance during the year I have been engaged in this study. I am indebted to my wife for many helpful suggestions while the manuscript was being written, to Mrs. S. Hart Moore for her most effective work in editing it, and to Agnes D. Peters who tirelessly and well presided over the manuscript's transformation into print. To all of these, and to the many other friends upon whom I have imposed, I give my thanks.

J.G.P.

CONTENTS

I

NIELLI

II

INTARSIAS

III

DRAWINGS

IV

COPPERPLATE ENGRAVINGS

LIST OF PLATES

The headings below show the relation of the plates to the various divisions of the text.

1. View of a Goldsmith's Shop. Detail from the copperplate engraving of the Planet Mercury. British Museum, London.

Nielli · Finiguerra · About 1452–1455

2 A. The Creation of Eve. Sulphur cast of a niello plaque. British Museum, London.

2 B. The Creation of Eve. Detail from a bronze relief on Ghiberti's second Baptistry doors (1452). Baptistry, Florence.

3 A. The Creation of Adam. Sulphur cast of a niello plaque. British Museum, London.

3 B. The Creation of Adam. Detail from a bronze relief on Ghiberti's second Baptistry doors (1452). Baptistry, Florence.

4 A. The Agony in the Garden. Sulphur cast of a niello plaque. Louvre (Rothschild collection), Paris.

4 B. The Agony in the Garden. Woodcut illustration from Bonaventura, *Meditationi sopra la Passione* (Venice, 1487), printed from a block of about 1450. Metropolitan Museum, New York.

5 A. The Ascension. Sulphur cast of a niello plaque. British Museum, London.

5 B. Christ in a Mandorla. Detail from the Burial of Saint Jerome. Painted by Fra Filippo Lippi (with the help of Fra Diamante) for the Duomo at Prato about 1453.

6. Three Women. Detail from the Miracle of Saint Ambrose. Painted by Fra Filippo Lippi in the 1440s. Kaiser Friedrich Museum, Berlin.

7 A. The Resurrection, and the Three Marys at the Tomb. Sulphur cast of a niello plaque. British Museum, London.

7 B. Group at the Foot of the Cross. Detail from the niello pax of the Crucifixion (Plate 9).

8. The Crucifixion. Terracotta relief. Presumably after a design made by Ghiberti about 1440–1450. Victoria and Albert Museum, London.

9. The Crucifixion. Niello pax. Made for the Florentine Baptistry. Bargello, Florence.

Nielli · Finiguerra and Pollaiuolo · About 1459–1464

10. Moses. Repoussé silver plaque (originally enameled) decorating a cross made for the Baptistry of Florence. Executed by Pollaiuolo between 1457 and 1459. Museo dell'Opera del Duomo, Florence.

11 A. Justice. Niello print. Louvre (Rothschild collection), Paris.

11 B. The Madonna and Child Enthroned between Saint Stephen and Saint Alban. Niello print. Louvre (Rothschild collection), Paris.

Nielli · Finiguerra, Pollaiuolo, and Baldini · About 1464–1465

49 A. Helen and Paris. Detail from the Picture-Chronicle. British Museum, London.

49 B. Personage. Detail from the copperplate engraving of the Triumph of Love (Plate 82). Albertina, Vienna.

50 A. A Prophet. Detail from the bronze enframement on Ghiberti's second Baptistry doors (1452). Baptistry, Florence.

50 B. Isaiah. Intarsia panel. Sacristy of the Duomo, Florence.

50 C. Hosea. Detail from the Picture-Chronicle. British Museum, London.

51 A. Maiden. Detail from the niello print of the Arming of Hector (Plate 12 B).

51 B. Amazon. Detail from the Picture-Chronicle. British Museum, London.

Copperplate Engravings · Pollaiuolo · About 1460–1462

52. The Battle of the Naked Men (The Dragon's Teeth). Copperplate engraving by Pollaiuolo. Metropolitan Museum, New York.

53 A. Bowman. Detail from Pollaiuolo's Battle of the Naked Men (Plate 52).

53 B. Hercules and the Hydra. Painted by Pollaiuolo. Uffizi, Florence.

54. Hercules and the Giants. Copperplate engraving. Designed by a late follower of Pollaiuolo, and executed by a North Italian master of the school of Mantegna about 1500. Metropolitan Museum, New York.

55 A. Detail from Pollaiuolo's Battle of the Naked Men (Plate 52).

55 B. Detail from the engraving of Hercules and the Giants (Plate 54).

56 A. Detail from the engraving of Hercules and the Giants (Plate 54). Executed by a North Italian master about 1500.

56 B. Detail from the copperplate engraving of Soldiers Carrying Trophies, from the series of the Triumphs of Caesar. North Italian, after a design by Andrea Mantegna, after 1492. British Museum, London.

56 C. Detail from Mantegna's copperplate engraving of the Risen Christ between Saint Andrew and Saint Longinus. Probably about 1500. Metropolitan Museum, New York.

56 D. Detail from the copperplate engraving of Hercules and Antaeus. Executed by Nicoletto Rosex da Modena, probably about 1500. British Museum, London.

Copperplate Engravings · Finiguerra and Pollaiuolo
About 1461–1462 and (from Plate 64 on) about 1461–1464

57. Combat Scene. Detail from the copperplate engraving of the Planet Mars. British Museum, London.

58 A. Boy Fishing. Detail from the copperplate engraving of the Planet Moon (see also Plate 59).

58 B. Seated Nude Youth. Niello print. Louvre (Rothschild collection), Paris.

59. Boys Fishing and Swimming. Detail from the copperplate engraving of the Planet Moon. British Museum, London.

60 A. Gymnasts. Detail from the copperplate engraving of the Planet Sun. British Museum, London.

60 B. Bathing Scene. Detail from the copperplate engraving of the Planet Venus. British Museum, London.

61. A Tilting Gallery and a Bathing Scene. Copperplate engraving. Executed by the Master of the Banderoles. Albertina, Vienna.

BIOGRAPHICAL NOTES

THE EARLY FLORENTINE DESIGNERS AND ENGRAVERS

Maso Finiguerra. Goldsmith, draughtsman, and engraver, born in Florence in 1426, died there in 1464. According to a note by Milanesi in his edition of Vasari's *Vite*, Finiguerra was buried in the church of Ognissanti on August 24 of that year. His father, who died in December of 1464, noted in his last testament that Maso was already dead.

Antonio Pollaiuolo. Goldsmith, sculptor, painter, draughtsman, and engraver, born in Florence, probably in 1433, died in Rome in 1498.

Baccio Baldini. Draughtsman and engraver, Florentine, active after the middle of the fifteenth century, died in 1487 (?).

Sandro Botticelli. Painter and draughtsman, born in Florence in 1445, died there in 1510.

Francesco Rosselli. Cartographer, miniaturist, engraver, and printer, born in Florence in 1445 or 1447, died before 1513.

OTHER FLORENTINE MASTERS MENTIONED IN THE TEXT

Lorenzo Ghiberti. Sculptor and goldsmith, born in Florence in 1378, died there in 1455.

Fra Filippo Lippi. Painter, born in Florence about 1406, died in Spoleto in 1469.

Alesso Baldovinetti. Painter and draughtsman, born in Florence, probably in 1425, died there in 1499.

Giuliano da Maiano. Architect and master woodworker, born at Maiano (near Settignano) in 1432, died in Naples in 1490.

Bartolommeo di Piero di Salì and *Betto di Francesco Betti*. Goldsmiths, active in Florence after the middle of the fifteenth century.

DEFINITIONS

Niello. For the purposes of this study, the term "niello" refers to a silver plate upon which a design was engraved with a burin. The engraved lines that cut into the plate's surface were filled with a black enamel-like substance called niello, from which the pieces so treated derived their name. The niello substance was composed of powdered silver, lead, copper, and sulphur, to which borax may have been added. It was applied to the silver in powdery form, and secured to it by the application of heat. The surface then was polished, and the design of the finished niello plate stood out in black against its silver background.

Sulphur Cast. The term "sulphur cast," or "sulphur," is used to describe an impression in sulphur taken from a plaster cast of an engraved silver plate before the lines were filled in with the niello substance. It presented the same engraved effect as the original.

Niello Print. The term "niello print" describes an impression on paper made by printing either from a niello plate before the black filling was added or from a sulphur cast of a niello plate. It is likely that both of these methods for making niello prints were used by early Florentine masters. The sole differences between a niello print and a copperplate print lie in the nature of the metal used, and in the fact that in the case of the niello print a sulphur cast of the silver plate may have served as intermediary.

I

NIELLI

DOCUMENTS AND REPORTS

Finiguerra

DOCUMENTS

1. Between 1452 and 1455 (and not necessarily in the year 1452 as has been believed) an entry was made in the *Libro grande dell'arte dei mercatanti* recording that a pax of silver, enameled and nielloed, was made for the Baptistry of Florence by Tommaso Finiguerra.

> Pace d'argento dorata smaltata e nielata di peso di o[ncie] 55 d[enari] 11 si fa per la Chiesa di S. Gio[vanni] per Tommaso di Finiguerra Orafo e si li paga a ragione di f[iorini] 1. largo l'oncia; costò in tutto f[iorini] 66.1–6. Libro d[etto] 200.
> • Archivio di Stato, Florence. Carte Strozziane, series II, no. 51, entitled *Fatti e memorie dell'arte dei mercatanti*, Vol. II, Ornamenti, carta 111, tergo.

2. On February 24, 1457, Antonio Finiguerra stated in a *catasto* (tax report) that his son Maso Finiguerra was then associated with Bartolommeo di Piero di Salì, a goldsmith.

> Tomaso mio figliuolo sopradetto è compagno di piero di Bartolomeo di salj horafo e non à nulla dicorpo e traghone per metà.
> • Archivio di Stato, Florence. Catasto, portate dell'anno 1457; quartiere di S. Maria Novella, gonfalone Unicorno; no. 813, no. 163.

REPORTS

1. On July 23, 1449, the painter Alesso Baldovinetti noted in his *Ricordi* that he exchanged a sulphur from the hand of Maso Finiguerra for another object.

> Ricevo da Bernardo d'Aghabito de'Ricci un pugnaletto in vendita, del quale pugniale gli debbo dare uno zolfo di mano di Tommaso Finiguerra tornito a sue spese, per grossi 6 d'argento ossia lira 1 . 13.

3

· From Alesso Baldovinetti, *Ricordi*, Libro A, carta 1, as quoted by Ruth Wedgwood Kennedy, in *Alesso Baldovinetti* (New Haven, 1938), p. 236.

2. In his *Trattato d'architettura*, written about 1460–1464, Filarete described Maso Finiguerra as a niellist among the several famous Italian masters who could take part in the decoration of an ideal high altar.

> ... l'ornamento poi dell'altare [è] tutto d'argento con molti intagli et ismalti bellissimi et ancora la tavola d'esso altare di molto maggiore prezzo perche è tutto d'oro con prete pretiose di gran valore la quale è fatta da solepnissimi maestri orefici e' quali capitorono in questa nostra citta nuovamente hedificata solo per la fama i quali furono di diverse parti d'Italia et fuori d'Italia franciosi todeschi et altri nomi io non so se none di questi nostri taliani uno che ebbe nome Mazzingho fiorentino et un altro che intagliava a niello bellissimo il quale ebbe nome Maso del Finiguerra et un altro che hebbe nome Giuliano che era chiamato Facchino et un altro che era chiamato Antonio del Pollaiuolo questi furno fiorentini ...
> · From Antonio Averlino Filarete, *Trattato d'architettura*, as quoted in *Filarete*, ed. Lazzaroni and Muñoz (Rome, 1908), p. 256.

3. In 1487 the Bolognese poet Salimbeni mentioned Finiguerra in describing the talents of the Bolognese master Francia as a niellist.

> Ma fra gli Orafi nostri io dirò il Franza
> Che io non lo scio lassar per maggior cura,
> Lui Polygnoto col pennello avanza
> E Phidia a l'operar de la sculptura,
> E col bollino ha tanta nominanza
> Che la sua a Maso Finiguerra obscura,
> A costui fo comparation di morti
> Perchè chi vive invidia al ver non porti.

> · From Salimbeni, *Epitalamio nelle pompe nuziali di Annibale Bentivoglio* (Bologna, 1487), as quoted by Adolfo Venturi, "La Pittura bolognese nel secolo XV," *Archivio storico dell'arte*, Vol. III (1890), p. 287.

4. In an undated letter Baccio Bandinelli (died 1560) stated that while working on the doors of the Baptistry of Florence, Ghiberti made use of youthful assistants, one of whom was Maso Finiguerra.

> ... per suo aiuto [Ghiberti] prese giovani con ottimo disegno, e fece due beni, opera mirabile e valenti maestri ... nel fare li giovani si feciono valenti, ... l'uno fu Maso Finiguerra ...
> · From Giovanni Bottari (& Stefano Ticozzi), *Raccolta di lettere* (Milan, 1822), Vol. I, pp. 104 f.

5. Vasari noted that Maso, famous for his work in niello, made some paxes for the Baptistry of Florence which were considered to be marvelous things.

Di questo lavorò mirabilissimamente Maso Finiguerra Fiorentino, il quale fu raro in questa professione, come ne fanno fede alcune paci di niello in san Giovanni di Fiorenza, che sono tenute mirabili.

· From Vasari, *Vite* (2nd ed.; Florence, 1568), Prima Parte, Della Pittura, Cap. xxxiii, *Del Niello*, p. 64.

6. Vasari also stated that there had never been any master of engraving and niello work who could make so great a number of figures as Maso could, whether in a small or large space, and cited as evidence certain paxes in the Baptistry of Florence that Maso wrought with minutely elaborated scenes from the Passion of Christ.

Era in questo tempo medesimo un altro Orefice chiamato Maso Finiguerra, il quale hebbe nome straordinario, & meritamente; che per lavorare di Bulino & fare di Niello non si era veduto mai, chi in piccoli, o in grandi spazij, facesse tanto numero di figure, quante ne faceva egli. Si come lo dimostrano ancora certe Paci, lavorate da lui in S. Giovanni di Fiorenza con istorie minutissime de la Passione di Cristo.

· From Vasari, *Vite* (2nd ed.; Florence, 1568), Seconda Parte, *Vita d'Antonio, & Piero Pollaiuoli*, p. 466.

7. Cellini stated that in the year 1515 there still lived a few old men who did nothing else but talk of the beauty of the art [of niello work] and of the great masters who had wrought in it, and above all of Finiguerra. At that time Cellini practiced the art with the examples of Finiguerra before him.

E se bene quando io andai a imparare l'arte della oreficeria, che fu nel mille cinquecento quindici, che così correvano gli anni della mia vita, sappiate che la detta arte d'intaglio di niello si era in tutto dismessa: ma perchè quei vecchi, che ancora vivevano, non facevano mai altro che ragionare della bellezza di quest'arte, e di quei buoni maestri che la facevano, e sopra tutto del Finiguerra; e perchè io ero molto volenteroso d'imparare, con grande studio mi messi a imparare, e con i begli esempli del Finiguerra io detti assai buon saggio di me.

· From Benvenuto Cellini, *I Trattati dell'oreficeria e della scultura* (Codice Marciano), ed. C. Milanesi (Florence, 1857), p. 14.

Pollaiuolo

DOCUMENTS

1. On February 22, 1457, Pollaiuolo and two other goldsmiths were commissioned to make a silver cross for the Baptistry of Florence.

Croce grande d'argento da farsi per il legno della Croce di N.S. per la chiesa di S. Giov. si dà a fare a Miliano di Dome Dei e Antonio di Jacopo Pollaiuolo Orefice la metà e l'altra metà a Betto di Franc° di Betto Orefice. Consegna d'argento fare detta croce.

· Archivio di Stato, Florence. Carte Strozziane, series II, no. 51, entitled *Fatti e memorie dell'arte dei mercatanti*, Vol. I, Deliberationi de' Consoli, 1455–1459, carta 216, recto (February 22, 1457).

2. A document of 1459 indicates that the cross was completed by that date, and that it was actually the work of two masters, Pollaiuolo and Betto Betti.

Una croce d'ariento tutta bianca fatta per la Chiesa di S. Giovanni Battista di peso l. 141, costò in tutto fior. 3036. 6. 18. 4, de' quali fior. 2006. 3. 13. 7, hebbe Antonio d'jacopo del Pollaiuolo e fior. 1030. 3. 5, Betto di Francesco Betti orafo.

· Archivio di Stato, Florence. Carte Strozziane, series II, no. 51, entitled *Fatti e memorie dell'arte dei mercatanti*, Vol. I, Libro grande dell'arte de' mercatanti, marked E, 1459, carta 10.

3. On January 3, 1460, the abbot of the Church of San Pancrazio in Florence commissioned Antonio Pollaiuolo and Bartolommeo di Piero di Salì to make a tabernacle or reliquary of silver for the arm of Saint Pancras.

Ricordo chome a di 3 di Gennaio 1459 (new style 1460) allogammo a ffare la riliquiera o vero tabernacolo dove s'à a mettere il braccio di messer San Pancratio . . . Allogammo a ffare detta reliquiera tutta d'ariento, sì come abbiamo avuto uno riccho et bello disegno, ad ANTONIO DI JACOPO et a BARTHOLOMEO DI PIERO SALI . . .

· Archivio di Stato, Florence. Conventi soppressi, no. 88: *Monastero vallombrosano di San Pancrazio*, register no. 63, carta 39, tergo, Reliquiera d'ariento pel braccio di messer San Pancratio.

Finiguerra and Pollaiuolo

DOCUMENTS

On various occasions between 1461 and 1464 both Finiguerra and Pollaiuolo received payments for independently making works in silver for Cino di Filippo di Messer Cino Rinuccini.

A dì 14 d'Aprile 1462 speso fior. 4 d.7, sono per un fornimento da cintola d'ariento ebbi da Maso Finiguerra, che pesò 0.3 d.23, lavorato di niello e di traforo, il quale feci mettere a una fetta paonazza, pesò detta fetta 0.2 d.3 in tutto fu 0.6 d.2, in conto al d.º Maso fior. 4. 7.

A dì 7 Luglio 1461 fior. 3. 4. 9 per valuta di d.50 d'ariento detti a Antonio de Pollaiuolo orafo, per uno fornimento d'ariento bianco da cintola con traforo e niello a 8 cignitoi, pesò 0.2, e la tolsi da lui per dare alla Ginevra che la donassi alla Sandra sua sirocchia, quando tornò a casa sua, come è d'usanza.

A dì 23 d'Agosto fior. 6. 10 pagai contanti a Maso Finiguerra orafo, sono per un fornimento alla parigina d'ariento dorato ebbi da lui per la d.ª Ginevra per portare bruno, pesò 0.4 d.8, e colla fetta, 0.6 d.9.

6

A dì 17 di Dicembre 1461. Si fanno buoni ai Rabatti fior. 6. 18. 6 che pagarono a Maso Finiguerra orafo, sono per un fornimento d'ariento, l'ha dorato e lavorato con traforo alla parigina, tolsi da lui per mettere a una fetta alla domaschina, pesò detto fornimento 0.4 d.9, e la fetta 0.3 d.19 in tutto 0.8 d.16, a ragione di fior. —6. 5 l'oncia.

A dì 20 di Febbraio. Fior. 8 a Maso Finiguerra, e sono per una dozzina di forchette d'ariento di peso 0.8, ebbi da lui per donare alla moglie di Niccolò Martelli, quando fece il fanciullo ch'ebbe nome Giovan Francesco.

A dì 6 Aprile 1462. Pagai contanti fior. —10. 8 a Antonio del Pollaiuolo orafo, sono per d. 2 di tremolanti e 2 catenelle d'ariento dorato, comprai da lui per la d.ª Ginevra per fare fruscoli a campanella.

A dì 2 di Luglio 1464. fior. 4. 4. 6. pagai a Maso d'Antonio Finiguerra orafo, sono per 5 cucchiai d'ariento comprai da lui, pesorono 0.5 d.6.

· From the *Ricordi di Cino di Filippo di Cino di Messer Francesco*, as quoted in *Ricordi storici di Filippo di Cino Rinuccini dal 1282 al 1460*, ed. G. Aiazzi (Florence, 1840), pp. 251 f.

REPORTS

1. Cellini stated that there was still in the Baptistry of Florence a silver pax "with a Crucifixion above, together with the two thieves, and with many ornaments of horses and other things." According to Cellini, Pollaiuolo was responsible for the pax's design and Finiguerra for its execution.

> . . . e si vede di sua mano [di Maso] una Pace con un Crocifisso dentrovi insieme con i dua ladroni, e con molti ornamenti di cavagli e di altre cose, fatta sotto il disegno di Antonio del Pollaiuolo già nominato di sopra, et è intagliata e niellata di mano del detto Maso: questo è d'argento in nel nostro bel San Giovanni di Firenze.
> · From Benvenuto Cellini, *I Trattati dell'oreficeria e della scultura* (Codice Marciano), ed. C. Milanesi (Florence, 1857), p. 13.

2. Cellini also stated that Maso Finiguerra pursued only the art of engraving nielli, that he had no rival in his profession, and that he always worked from the designs of Pollaiuolo.

> Maso Finiguerra fece l'arte solamente dello intagliare di niello; questo fu un uomo che mai non ebbe nissuno paragone di quella cotale professione, e sempre operò servendosi dei disegni del detto Antonio [Pollaiuolo].
> · From Benvenuto Cellini, *I Trattati dell'oreficeria e della scultura* (Codice Marciano), ed. C. Milanesi (Florence, 1857), p. 7.

PART 2

FINIGUERRA

There can be no doubt that in his day Maso Finiguerra was renowned as a master of the art of niello work. In his *Trattato*, written about 1460–1464, the sculptor and goldsmith Filarete described him as a master who engraved beautiful niello plaques; and in 1487, twenty-three years after Maso's death, a poet named Salimbeni compared the fame of a Bolognese goldsmith and niellist, Francia, with that of the Florentine master. Various records support these fifteenth-century opinions. We learn from one that in 1449, when Maso was twenty-three years old, he was already producing nielli; and from a document datable between 1452 and 1455 that he made a nielloed pax for the Florentine Baptistry. Then there are the sixteenth-century reports by the Florentine goldsmith and sculptor Cellini, who on various occasions referred to Maso as a celebrated niellist, and who specifically stated that Finiguerra and Pollaiuolo together made a pax of the Crucifixion for the Baptistry of Florence. Vasari, Cellini's contemporary, also described Maso as a master of niello work who produced various paxes for the Florentine Baptistry.

Such, as we begin this study, is the evidence directly connecting Finiguerra with the niellist's art. One other report, not directly concerned with niello work but bearing on Maso's early career, and therefore of possible significance, may also be noted at this time. It occurs in a letter written by another contemporary of Cellini, Baccio Bandinelli, whose father was a goldsmith, and it indicates that Finiguerra assisted Ghiberti in the making of the Baptistry doors.

In the pages that follow we shall attempt to erect an orderly structure on the foundations of these brief notices. We shall begin by seeking to discover a niellist in whose work the influences of Ghiberti and Pollaiuolo may be identified. For it would seem apparent that if by any chance both Bandinelli and Cellini were right, and if confirmation of their testimoney is indeed available, it would occur in nielli referable to Maso Finiguerra.

Ghiberti died in 1455, three years after he had completed the famous "Gates of Paradise," and it is two years later, in 1457, that we first find a notice of Pollaiuolo's activity as a goldsmith. So if Maso had worked with these two masters, he would first have been with Ghiberti, possibly continuing with him until the death of the great sculptor-goldsmith in 1455. Soon thereafter, in 1456, Finiguerra himself became a master goldsmith. It is in the period between 1456 and 1464, when he died, that we shall look for indications that he collaborated with Antonio Pollaiuolo.

8

To begin with the Ghibertian period: we have unfortunately little to go on in the way of notable pieces. But what there is, is most revealing. Our chief source of evidence is a famous series of sulphur casts. Seven of these tiny compositions are scenes from the Creation, and these are all in the British Museum. In addition there are the fourteen scenes from the Passion: nine in the British Museum and five in the Rothschild collection in the Louvre. All of these Creation and Passion sulphurs seem to have been made by the same master and to have originally formed part of the decoration for a small Florentine altarpiece. According to Luigi Lanzi (*Storia pittorica della Italia*, 1809, Vol. I, p. 90), they were so used in the Convent of the Carmelites in Florence.

The Ghibertian sulphurs in this group are the Creation scenes, for their compositions are largely based on details of the bronze reliefs from Ghiberti's second Baptistry doors. The Creation of Adam (Pl. 3 A) and the Creation of Eve (Pl. 2 A), two of the sulphur casts, are taken from details of the bronze relief of the Creation of Adam and Eve (Pls. 3 B and 2 B). Other of the sulphurs, such as Cain and Abel Worshiping before an Altar, also find their prototypes on the Ghiberti doors.

Now the interesting thing is that in contrast with the Creation sulphurs those of the Passion show no compositional affiliations with Ghibertian models. And this could hardly have been otherwise, for the panels on the Ghiberti doors illustrated only Old Testament scenes.

How, then, are we to account for the Passion designs, if they are indeed the work of Finiguerra? The answer is not an easy one, nor is there any reason why it should be, for as we shall gradually discover during the course of our study Finiguerra's artistic personality was a complicated one. In the present instance it seems, on the basis of evidence available to us, that the artist responsible for the series — whom we provisionally identify as Finiguerra — drew upon two principal sources for his Passion designs.

One source was the series of illustrations in a famous block book representing the Passion, which had been executed in Venice — very probably about the year 1450 (Prince d'Essling, *Les Livres à figures vénitiens*, Florence, 1907, Part I, Vol. I, nos. 1–18). It is the earliest Italian book with printed illustrations; and, although Venetian as to detail, the general composition of the individual prints would seem to depend on earlier German engravings, whether on wood or metal. One of these woodcuts, the Agony in the Garden (Pl. 4 B), seems to have given Finiguerra the plan for his version of the subject (Pl. 4 A), as for instance in the placement of each of his four major figures. As we shall presently see, this German-inspired block-book Passion has an important place in the annals of Florentine engraving, for it continued to be a source of inspiration for the early Florentine niellists (Section I, Part 4) and print makers (Section IV, Part 5).

A second source upon which the designer drew in the planning of the Passion nielli was Fra Filippo Lippi, a Florentine contemporary; his work, like that of Ghiberti, provided our master with a variety of models.

Take, for example, the sulphurs of the Ascension and the Three Marys at the Tomb. In the Ascension (Pl. 5 A) the risen Christ would seem to be stylistically dependent upon the figure of Christ in Filippo's painting of the Burial of Saint Jerome (Pl. 5 B; Mary Pittaluga, *Filippo Lippi*, Florence, 1949, pl. 75). Dr. Pittaluga and various other critics hold that the painting, which is in the Duomo at Prato, was executed about 1453. As we shall discover below, this was just about the time when Finiguerra would have been at work on the series of nielli of which the Ascension is one of the casts. In the panel of the Three Marys at the Tomb (Pl. 7 A), the Mary whose back is turned toward us would seem to be based on a figure in another of Fra Filippo's paintings, the Miracle of Saint Ambrose (Pittaluga, *op. cit.*, pl. 36), a work of the 1440s that until the last war was in the Kaiser Friedrich Museum in Berlin. A comparison of details of pose and drapery (Pl. 6) surely leaves little room for uncertainty as to the source of the niello design.

Apart from the Passion sulphurs, there is one other important early work in which the same Filippesque manner is to be observed — a nielloed silver pax of the Crucifixion in the Bargello (Pl. 9). This instance is all the more convincing since it borrows from a source also used in the Passion series: pose for pose, and fold for fold in drapery, the central figure of Mary in the plaque of the Three Marys at the Tomb (Pl. 7 A) finds its exact parallel in the Mary of the Crucifixion pax (Pl. 7 B).

The influence of Ghiberti — one of the lines of evidence leading us to Maso Finiguerra — is also to be discerned in this pax, for, as Richard Krautheimer has pointed out to me, its composition as a whole seems to derive from a relief by that sculptor. Ghiberti's original creation has been lost, but a terracotta of the subject (Pl. 8), which may have been made in the Ghiberti workshop, exists in the Victoria and Albert Museum (no. 5786–1859 in the *Catalogue of Italian Sculpture* by Eric Maclagan and Margaret H. Longhurst, London, 1932, p. 15). The general plan of its composition, and specifically the way of representing the three crosses and the figures upon them, are so closely followed in the niello plaque that there would seem to be no doubt as to the origin of the latter's design. In the case of the pax, therefore, the influences of both Lippi and Ghiberti are found combined in a single piece. Weighty evidence, it may be felt, that one designer — Finiguerra — who was influenced by both of these masters produced the Crucifixion pax as well as the series of the Creation and Passion sulphurs.

Other evidence supports the attribution of the pax to Finiguerra. Ghiberti's doors were finally set up in 1452, and it hardly seems likely that Maso, as an assistant in the great sculptor's shop, would have used the designs for his Creation series before they were in the public domain. It would seem probable that Maso produced the companion Creation and Passion nielli and the Crucifixion pax during the years subsequent to the unveiling of the doors. Not much later, however, for in another five years or so he would be beginning to work in collaboration with Pollaiuolo. So about 1452, or shortly thereafter, would be a reasonable time for Finiguerra to have made them. And as we know from the Mercatanzia document (*Libro grande dell'arte dei mercatanti*), it was during the period of 1452–1455 that Maso made a nielloed pax for the Baptistry of Florence. On the evidence of both style and chronology, we may therefore identify the Bargello pax of the Crucifixion as the one recorded as being Maso's work. Such as it is then — and our evidence is admittedly restricted to a few pieces — this is what we can conjecture regarding the early pre-Pollaiuolan works of Maso Finiguerra.

As we shall discover when we come to consider the later nielli, and in particular when we study the Florentine Picture-Chronicle, the Ghibertian influence in Finiguerra's work was no mere youthful aspect of the niellist's career, one that would vanish when the master came into contact with other influences. We shall indeed see that the Picture-Chronicle, Finiguerra's final work and his masterpiece, can only be fully understood in the light of its intimate relationship to the Ghibertian style. No less significantly, we shall also see that Filippesque traces will continually recur as a leitmotiv throughout the later nielli and the Chronicle drawings, in a manner closely paralleling the Finiguerra-Ghiberti relationship.

PART 3

FINIGUERRA AND POLLAIUOLO

From the testimony of both Cellini and Vasari, particularly that of the former, we may be sure that Finiguerra and Pollaiuolo worked together. In 1515 when the young goldsmith Benvenuto Cellini was learning how to make nielli, he had the examples of Finiguerra before him. At that time, according to Cellini, "a few old men still living did nothing but talk of the beauty of the art [of niello work] and of the great masters who had wrought in it, & above all of Finiguerra." Since Cellini learned about Maso from men who had actually known him — doubtless goldsmiths like himself — he would seem to be a highly trustworthy source of information.

Cellini reported that Maso always worked on the basis of designs by Antonio Pollaiuolo, and he described a Crucifixion pax in the Florentine Baptistry as having

11

been designed by Antonio and engraved by Maso. Vasari gave other indication that they worked together when he wrote that Maso was a good draughtsman, but that in competition with him, Antonio equaled him in diligence and surpassed him in drawing.

Judging from these accounts, one can reasonably say that the two young goldsmiths must have been employed in the same workshop. There are, in fact, documents which show that both Maso and Antonio belonged to the goldsmith's bottega of one Bartolommeo di Piero di Salì. Although Finiguerra is recorded as being there in 1457, and Pollaiuolo in 1460, there is no record to show when either of them commenced working with Di Salì. There are, however, documents revealing that at various times between 1461 and 1464 both men received payments for independently making objects in silver for a Cino Rinuccini; therefore they may have been in the same shop from at least 1460 to 1464.

In setting out to find nielli made by this combination, we must know what to look for. We shall first seek stylistic evidence that will form a link between various examples of niello work and works of art known definitely to have been designed by Pollaiuolo. With that as a basis, we can proceed to re-examine such a group of Pollaiuolan nielli for any stylistic elements that may be referable to Maso Finiguerra, for we have already seen him to be a designer in his own right, although, to be sure, a derivative one. In the course of this examination we shall also look for technical evidence to reveal Maso's hand as that of the engraver.

It is a strange fact that there is only one work executed by Pollaiuolo before 1464 concerning which there is no question as to authenticity or date. This is the silver cross made for the Baptistry of Florence. It becomes the touchstone for the attribution to Pollaiuolo of the designs for various nielli and niello derivatives.

On April 30, 1457, Antonio Pollaiuolo and two other Florentine goldsmiths were commissioned to make a cross for the Baptistry, which is now in the Museo dell'Opera del Duomo. One of Antonio's two associates apparently soon gave up his share in the enterprise, for the cross as it appeared when finished in 1459 represented the work of two men: Betto di Francesco Betti, who was seemingly responsible for the upper section; and Pollaiuolo, to whom the lower section seems to have been intrusted.

Antonio's section is decorated with fifteen plaquettes of repoussé silver in various shapes and sizes. These were originally enameled, but the enamel has long since fallen away, leaving as silvery skeletons the basic structures of the various compositions. Although the silver parts also have suffered from the ravages of time, these plaquettes show a consistent style — one that is masculine, driving, nervous. Since it may be assumed that the designs were planned shortly after the commission was received, they give a good idea of what was probably Pollaiuolo's style about the year 1457. They show that his career was by then already under way.

One of the best preserved of these reliefs depicts Moses (Pl. 10), a powerful figure, in which some authors claim to see anticipations of the prophets in the ceiling of the Sistine Chapel. For this study it is enough to show that the Moses serves as a starting point for establishing a series of nielli made after the designs of Pollaiuolo.

In the illustrations, the Moses and the first of our group of nielli, the print of Justice from the Rothschild collection in the Louvre, are placed in confrontation (Pls. 10 and 11 A), for they undeniably have much in common. Since the design of the niello print of Justice is the mirror image of a lost silver plaque, I describe and illustrate it in reverse, so that its original composition can be visualized and a comparison with the Moses be made with a minimum of distortion.

Viewed in reverse manner, Justice is seated beneath a canopy held aloft by two winged putti, and gazes to her left. In her right hand she holds a sword, in her left, a globe. Covering the lower part of her high-waisted gown, a heavy robe falls in clearly marked decorative folds. Her right foot is seen almost in full profile beneath the hem of this robe, and there is a glimpse of her left foot, delicately flexed at the instep. At either side of Justice, two small bears as heraldic supporters display armorials of the Orsini. (Unfortunately no connection has so far been found between this niello print and any member of that family.) Winged putti heads at the sides and base complete the design.

Moses has the same seated pose, the same haughty half turn of the head, the same robe with its characteristic folds, and the same position of the feet. In addition to details such as these, the general effect is the same. These several resemblances, both specific and general, would seem to indicate that the Justice also was after a design by Pollaiuolo.

A further, although indirect, indication of this results from a comparison of the niello Justice with the painted panel of the same subject by Antonio's brother, Piero Pollaiuolo. This work, which is now in the Uffizi, was executed about 1470 for the courtroom of the Mercatanzia in Florence. Although it has been so largely restored that its painterly qualities are indeterminable, it would seem to be a later and more mature development of the Pollaiuolan composition of Justice as represented in the niello print.

Among the various pieces stylistically related to the Justice print is the Madonna and Child Enthroned between Saint Stephen and Saint Alban (Pl. 11 B). Not only is the Virgin posed much as Justice is, and garbed in a similar heavy robe, but also the canopy over her head is nearly identical with that of the Justice print, and the winged putti appearing in both prints are practically brothers. Two other prints in this group of stylistically related nielli are the Arming of Hector (Pl. 12 B) and Hector and Achilles (Pl. 14 A). Both seem to be incidents from a Trojan War series that once may have ornamented a casket or some other object of domestic use made for a wealthy Florentine. When the maiden who is helping Hector buckle on his colletin

13

is compared with the figure of Justice, her Pollaiuolan character becomes evident: we note the same facial features and coiffures, a similar treatment of draperies, and the same aware and vivid draughtsmanship.

Closely related to these two compositions is a print of the Crucifixion in the Rothschild collection in the Louvre (Pl. 16). Its silver original is lost, but there is a silver variant in the Bargello, which will be discussed in Part 4 of this Section, and there is also a variant niello print in the Metropolitan Museum. On Plate 14 B a detail of the Louvre print is shown next to that of the two struggling warriors, Hector and Achilles. So telling is the consonance of style that there would seem to be little doubt that this Crucifixion composition is another item to be added to our growing list of examples of niello designs by Pollaiuolo. More than that, it would seem to be the composition for the pax "with a Crucifixion above, together with the two thieves, and with many ornaments of horses and other things," which according to Cellini was engraved for the Baptistry by Finiguerra after Pollaiuolo's design.

The pax described by Cellini was unquestionably a celebrated example of quattro-cento goldsmith's work. And the pax that was the original of the Louvre print was surely a well-known piece, for the existence of two variants — one in silver and the other in a niello print — speaks for its popularity in its own time. It was surely worthy of Cellini's citation, for as we may judge from the moving detail of the swooning Madonna (Pl. 15) we are concerned with an object insignificant only in linear measurement.

The significance of this attribution is that it at once places Finiguerra actively in the story. So far he has been a silent partner, one whose presence was only to be blindly assumed. But here, presumably, is a pax which Cellini records as the combined work of the two men. When from the standpoint of technique we examine all the niello prints so far considered in this study, we find that the actual work of engraving seems to have been done by a single hand. We may, therefore, subject to further findings, tentatively conclude that all the nielli represented, the pre-Pollaiuolan sulphurs considered in Part 2 as well as the pieces now under consideration, were engraved by Maso Finiguerra.

Among the works related in style to the Crucifixion is the Coronation of the Virgin, the composition of which is known on silver, sulphur, and paper. Although the silver pax that is seemingly the original of the composition is in the Bargello, the sulphur cast of it in the British Museum (Pl. 17) strangely enough gives a far better idea of the niello's original quality. Owing probably to repeated cleaning and polishing, the silver surface of the Bargello pax is worn down; the sulphur on the other hand is miraculously fresh, and it shows as does no other example what a Florentine niello must have looked like in its original state.

Another pax composition, that of the Baptism of Christ, is related to the Coronation of the Virgin. A silver plaque of this subject — possibly it may be the original

14

example — was formerly in the Figdor collection. And there is a fine reproduction of the composition in the niello print from the Salamanca-Rothschild series in the Louvre (Pl. 18).

What, you may ask, is the relationship of the Baptism design to that of the Coronation of the Virgin? For one thing, the kneeling saints in the foreground are almost identical with those found in the Coronation piece. And, for another, the figure of Saint John finds its twin among the Coronation's crowd of saints. All this would seem to indicate that the Baptism design belongs with this group of Pollaiuolan nielli. Moreover, it would seem to be related to the Baptism plaque in silver repoussé from Pollaiuolo's cross of 1457–1459. Although the repoussé plaque is the finer thing, its figure of Christ being drawn more sensitively and at the same time more powerfully than the nielloed one, that is only to be expected since the former was Antonio's own handiwork, whereas the latter represented a collaborative undertaking.

Still another niello print to be attributed to the Finiguerra-Pollaiuolo partnership is the Seated Nude Youth in the Rothschild collection (Pl. 19 A), the figure being drawn in the same way as that of Christ in the Baptism print. The like treatment of leg and foot in each instance is particularly to be noted. Once we realize that this print may have been made from a design by Pollaiuolo shortly after 1460, we see how rare it really is, for it is one of the first "studio" designs of the nude — the ancestor of endless progeny. It calls to mind the observation of Vasari that as a young man Pollaiuolo "had a more modern grasp of the nude than the masters before his day," the result of his having "dissected many bodies in order to study their anatomy."

Among the other niello prints associated with this group is the one representing a Schoolmaster Surrounded by His Pupils (Pl. 12 A), surely a masterpiece of its genre. Then there are the Cain and Abel (Pl. 19 c) and the Sacrifice of Abraham (Pl. 21), two prints of key importance for our study since they give us a clear-cut indication of the complex system that was followed in the designing of nielli. In the former print, the figures of Cain and Abel are after designs by Pollaiuolo, but the composition, in the Finiguerran manner, is based on one of Ghiberti's reliefs for the Baptistry doors (Pl. 19 B). It may be noted, incidentally, that the landscape with the walled city in the background is almost identical with that found in the Baptism of Christ (Pl. 18). In the print of the Sacrifice of Abraham, the two figures in the foreground are seemingly after Pollaiuolan models. The composition as a whole, however, is clearly borrowed from another of Ghiberti's reliefs (Pl. 20). The donkey is unquestionably a copy of Ghiberti's, and the actual Sacrifice of Abraham, a weakly designed thing, recalls the Creation series of sulphur casts in the British Museum, which we have already attributed to Finiguerra.

At this point we may briefly take stock of the situation. So far, we have for stylistic reasons isolated under the name of Pollaiuolo what seems to be a closely related series of compositions. For the sake of clarity we have purposely not given a full stylistic analysis of all the examples cited. Some of these, however, reveal a quality of design that is not entirely Pollaiuolan. And we now have seen in the prints of Cain and Abel and of the Sacrifice of Abraham that Finiguerra shared with Pollaiuolo the designer's task.

Since this is so in one instance, our problem is to determine if possible how general was this collaboration and the nature of Maso's share in it. We now present evidence to suggest that Finiguerra may have actively participated in the development of practically all the designs on which Pollaiuolo worked.

In the Baptism print (Pl. 18), which has already been studied, the nude figure of the Christ is depicted without the wealth of anatomical detail that so marks Pollaiuolo's engraved print of the Battle of the Naked Men (Pl. 52). The niello Christ is a tiny figure about two inches high; that is to say, it is about one-fifth the height of the warriors in the large Battle print. The niello figure is treated in a simple but powerful manner that would seem to be a practical compromise between the contrary demands of space and style. It seems logical that it would have been the engraver, Finiguerra, who, as the expert in niello work, saw the need for and actually effected such a compromise.

Previously we observed how Finiguerra had occasion to borrow ideas from the paintings of Fra Filippo Lippi. We now see a repetition of the same situation in various nielli in the group presently under discussion. To be specific we see this Filippesque influence in the niello print of the Schoolmaster Surrounded by His Pupils (Pl. 12 A), for the central figure of the teacher is clearly in the manner of the great painter. It may be compared with the Saint Damiano from the panel of the Madonna and Child and Four Saints in the Uffizi (M. Pittaluga, *Filippo Lippi*, pl. 38), a work of the 1440s. We see this same Filippesque note in the niello print of the Arming of Hector (Pl. 12 B), for the maidens in classical dress at either side of the warrior are certainly closely related to the serving-woman in Filippo's painting of the Madonna and Child with Stories from the Life of Saint Anne (Pittaluga, *op. cit.*, pl. 67), a work of the early 1450s. Then, too, the maiden kneeling at the warrior's feet may similarly be compared with the angel at the lower right in Lippi's Coronation of the Virgin (Pittaluga, *op. cit.*, pl. 31), which had been painted in the 1440s (Pl. 13 A and B). To mention one other instance, we also see this reflection of Fra Filippo in the sulphur cast of the Coronation of the Virgin (Pl. 17), the whole composition of which is derived from Lippi's painting of the subject. This great panel had been ordered for the Florentine church of Sant'Ambrogio, and the bishop saint himself is represented in it, standing at the extreme left. It may not be without significance that one of the two kneeling bishops in the foreground of the sulphur cast may also be Ambrogio, for he is seemingly identified by the name on his collar.

16

Such a dependence upon the works of Filippo Lippi clearly parallels that found in the nielli made by Finiguerra prior to the latter's association with Pollaiuolo. Certainly no such relation to Filippo is to be found in any of Pollaiuolo's repoussé plaques for the Baptistry cross of 1457–1459 nor in his only other dated early work, the panels of the Baptistry embroideries, which were commissioned in 1466. We may reasonably conclude then that these Filippesque elements are an indication of Finiguerra's participation with Pollaiuolo in the development of the niello designs.

Granted that the two men did in fact collaborate as designers, the question remains: just how did they work together? It is my feeling that Finiguerra may have suggested the compositions and, on the basis of designs then supplied to him by Pollaiuolo, set down the completed compositions upon the silver plates. Be that as it may, as the engraver, Maso would certainly have always had the last word as to a design's character. Our best evidence in favor of such a method of collaboration in design will be met with later, when in Section IV, Part 3, we consider the Planets, a series of prints that from the stylistic evidence seem to have been designed in just such a manner.

As for the dating of the various nielli with which we have been concerned, one can offer no more than terminal figures. The niello print of Justice, which follows the same general composition as the plaque of Moses from the Baptistry cross completed by Pollaiuolo in 1459, could hardly have been made before that year. And it would seem doubtful if any of the Pollaiuolo-Finiguerra nielli were made prior to the Justice. If our theory of their joint authorship is right, none of them could have been made after the midsummer of 1464, when Finiguerra died. All these nielli, therefore, would seem to fall within the brief five-year span of about 1459–1464.

PART 4

FINIGUERRA, POLLAIUOLO, AND BALDINI

Finiguerra and Pollaiuolo do not seem to have worked together entirely unassisted. Other masters were surely with these two, chief among them being the goldsmith Baccio Baldini, who on various occasions was their collaborator in print making. As we shall now discover, Baldini also worked with both Finiguerra and Pollaiuolo in the creation of nielli.

Our chief evidence is the series of twenty plaques that decorate a silver-gilt cross in The Metropolitan Museum of Art. This is one of the finest known series of nielli, and it represents the Florentine school richly and completely. If the cross

17

itself is not a spectacular thing, it must be remembered that because of the diminutive size of the plaques, it was necessarily keyed to a minor scale. Within the limits of that scale, however, it is a superb example of renaissance goldsmithery.

Very likely the cross was made for use during processions, for both its front and back are fully decorated (Pls. 22 and 23), and it compares in shape and appearance with the cross held by the figure of Faith (Pl. 26 B), one of the repoussé plaques on Pollaiuolo's Baptistry cross of 1457–1459. The front surface lacks its sculptured crucifix, of which nothing is known, although surely it was made of silver. A small reliquary window above the space reserved for the crucifix once contained a fragment of the True Cross, for above it is an inscription reading LIGNUM CRUCIS. The terminal plaques of the four arms represent the Mourning Virgin (Pl. 26 A), Saint John (Pls. 28 and 32 A), the Magdalen (Pl. 27 A), and the Agony in the Garden (Pl. 29 A). The Franciscan in the tiny plaque above the Magdalen is Saint Anthony of Padua. Five other, minor plaques served as the background for the missing crucifix: two of these are mourning angels; two show the eclipsed sun and moon; the fifth is a simple, diapered pattern.

The back of the cross is apparently in its original condition, the center occupied by a large plaque of the crucified Christ (Pl. 24). Here the four terminal plaques represent the Flagellation (Pl. 25 A), the Crowning with Thorns (Pl. 25 B), the Pietà (Pl. 29 B), and the Last Supper (Pls. 30 A and B, and 31 B). Saint Francis and Saint Clare are at either side of Christ; below Him is Saint Bernadino of Siena, and above Him is found the pelican, symbol of the Eucharist.

The base, or "shoe," of the cross bears a partly legible Italian inscription revealing for whom the cross was originally made. The part that can be read may be translated as follows: "This cross is made for the Poor Sisters of Santa Chiara . . ." That the cross was indeed executed for a convent of the Poor Clares is indicated by the nielli themselves. Four of them, as we have seen, show saints of the monastic orders: three of these are Franciscans, and the other — facing Saint Francis in a position of honor — is Saint Clare, his devoted follower.

There is good reason to believe that the convent of the Poor Clares here mentioned was in Florence. In the year 1450, Pope Nicholas V had sanctioned the founding of such a convent in that city, and it may be assumed, given the custom of religious orders, that this one was quickly established. Its site in Florence has not been ascertained, but we do know that in the year 1490 the convent was relocated next to the Annalena, where it remained in active operation until the beginning of the nineteenth century. Thereafter it was used as a school until 1861, when the building was closed and the contents sold. It is possible that the cross may have come upon the market at the time of the convent's final dissolution.

The cross first came to public attention in the Düsseldorf exhibition of 1902 (*Catalogue*, no. 2190); it was then in the Thewalt collection in Cologne. In 1903 it was sold at auction to Julius Campe of Hamburg (*Kunstsammlung Karl Thewalt*, Lempertz sale, Cologne, 1903, no. 985, pl. 16), and shortly thereafter was purchased by J. Pierpont Morgan, who lent it to the Victoria and Albert Museum in London. The cross came to the Metropolitan Museum as a gift from Mr. Morgan in 1917. It was described by Marc Rosenberg (*Niello*, Frankfurt am Main, 1925, pp. 87–89) as Florentine; by Cyril Bunt (*Burlington Magazine*, LXV, 1934, pp. 26 ff.) as made by Pollaiuolo about 1480; by Attilio Sabatini (*Antonio e Piero del Pollaiuolo*, Florence, 1944, p. 100) as a work close to the Passion engravings (which as we shall presently see was a very good guess); and by Sergio Ortolani (*Il Pollaiuolo*, Milan, 1948, p. 167) as being in a generalized Pollaiuolan style.

We now turn to the question of authorship. As in our examination of the nielli in Part 3, we shall first seek to associate a number of the cross's plaques with the style of Pollaiuolo. Then we shall endeavor to determine the parts played by Finiguerra and Baldini in this enterprise. Our discussion will consider the larger, more important plaques: the eight "terminal" nielli, and the crucified Christ.

To begin with Pollaiuolo, evidence of his participation is seemingly to be found on many of the plaques; for example, in the Flagellation (Pl. 25 A) a definitely Pollaiuolan treatment of the body of Christ can be noted. This is the same heavy, muscular body that we have already seen in the figure of Christ in the Baptism print (Pl. 18), the design of which was related to Pollaiuolo in the foregoing Part of this study. Incidentally, the curious method of flooring (to be seen also in the Crowning with Thorns, Pl. 25 B, and the Last Supper, Pl. 30 A), in which the platform is represented as a panel with a clearly finished edge at the front, and with its surface marked checkerboard fashion in perspective, is found in the niello print of the Schoolmaster Surrounded by His Pupils (Pl. 12 A), the design of which has already been attributed to the Finiguerra-Pollaiuolo combination.

Additional signs that Pollaiuolo was one of the designers at work on this cross are seen in the Mourning Virgin (Pl. 26 A), which may be compared with the figure of Faith (Pl. 26 B) on the Baptistry cross executed by Pollaiuolo between 1457 and 1459. The silhouettes of both figures are similar; similar also is the use of the drapery. Perhaps even more telling is the Magdalen (Pl. 27 A). At first glance the plaque on which she appears seems to be the least Pollaiuolan niello on the Museum's cross; however, she has a definite relationship to the standing figure of a woman (Pl. 27 B) from the embroidered panel of Zacharias Writing the Name of the Baptist, one of a series of embroideries designed by Pollaiuolo for the Baptistry. There can, I feel, be no doubt that in both the niello Magdalen and the embroidery figure the treatment of the draperies is very similar. The mantles fall with the same rhythmic sequence of folds over the raised right arms, and they are caught up and held in the same characteristic fashion by the left hands. The hands, too, seem alike — long, graceful, and full, emerging from tight, narrow sleeves.

19

So it is that one of the nielli on the Metropolitan's cross is stylistically related to a niello pax believed to have been designed by Pollaiuolo, and two others are shown to relate to details of the Baptistry cross and the Baptistry embroideries, both of which are documented works by the master. Other of the plaques would seem to show a similar style, among them the Christ crucified. Admittedly there is no existing Pollaiuolan equivalent for it. We know, however, that Antonio had painted a Crucifixion for the Compagnia di Sant'Angelo in Arezzo. If the painting is early (we do not know when it was made), the niello may be a reflection of its design. At any event, as a comparison with the bronze Christ in the Santo at Padua will indicate, it is strongly Donatellan, and Pollaiuolo's style, as is known, was based to some extent on that of Donatello.

With respect to Maso Finiguerra, he would seem (as in the instance of the nielli described above in Part 3) to have been concerned with the development of all the designs for the cross on which his associate Pollaiuolo was working. For example, the features and the draperies of Saint John (Pl. 28) recall those of the man seated at the small table at the right in Fra Filippo Lippi's Banquet of Herod, a work executed in the early sixties for the Duomo at Prato (Pittaluga, *Filippo Lippi*, pl. 127). Now such a Filippesque element is not to be found in any independently produced design by Pollaiuolo; whereas, as we have seen in Parts 2 and 3, it does occur in works designed by Finiguerra. The Magdalen (Pl. 27 A) also, despite the presence of Pollaiuolan qualities already noted here, has the features of a Lippi Madonna, such as the Virgin of the Annunciation in the Palazzo Doria in Rome, a work somewhat earlier than the Banquet of Herod (Pittaluga, *op. cit.*, pl. 64).

In addition to Maso's general and apparently supervisory interest in the designs of this group of nielli, it seems likely that two of the compositions may have stemmed fairly directly from him: the Agony in the Garden, and the Last Supper. The most immediate connection of the Agony in the Garden (Pl. 29 A) would seem to be with the pre-Pollaiuolan nielli of Finiguerra, particularly with the sulphur casts of the Passion series (Section I, Part 2). For example, the central kneeling figure in the sulphur Ascension (Pl. 5 A) appears to bear a close stylistic resemblance to Christ in the Agony in the Garden. The Last Supper (Pls. 30 A and B, and 31 B) also would seem to hark back to Maso's pre-Pollaiuolan past, and to reveal use of a design from the block-book *Passion of Our Lord* of about 1450 (Pl. 31 A).

Interestingly enough, the Last Supper alone of all the cross's nielli, and for that matter alone of all the early Florentine nielli, bears a cypher in which the letters A, B, and L may be distinguished. Even if the reading of the letters A and L is not certain, there can be no doubt that the chief letter in the cypher is a clear and definite B. Since, if we do not err in our attribution of the designs, it cannot refer to either of the two designers, it follows then that it must refer to the engraver.

The engraver of the cross's plaques appears to be a master whose technique differs basically from Finiguerra's. Although engraved in a highly skilled manner, the nielli on the Metropolitan's cross show in comparison with those attributed to Finiguerra a certain loss of fluidity in the translation of design to metal. The touch is that of a more heavily muscled, less nervous hand. I submit that Baccio Baldini, who is described by Vasari as having followed Finiguerra, was the only Florentine goldsmith then active to whose name the cypher with its clear-cut B could possibly have applied. At this time, however, I do no more than name Baldini as the engraver of the cross's plaques. Later in our study we shall consider the relation of these nielli to the copperplate engravings believed on the basis of other evidence to have been made by Baldini.

In concluding our study of the Metropolitan's cross, it may be noted that since Finiguerra had a share in its design, work on it must have commenced as early as 1464. On the other hand, because of its relationship from the standpoint of engraving to the second series of the Planets (details, Pl. 84 A and B), which as we shall presently see were executed by Baldini in 1464–1465, it may also be dated as late as 1465. Hence, "about 1464–1465" would seem accurately to place it.

Another important example of niello work of the period of the Metropolitan's cross can also be attributed to the hand of Baldini. In the preceding Part 3 on Finiguerra and Pollaiuolo, we described the niello print (Pl. 16) after a pax of the Crucifixion which may be presumed to be by the two partners on the basis of Cellini's statement. At that time we mentioned a silver variant of the composition in the Bargello (Pl. 33). When the engraving style of this Bargello pax is compared with that of the Metropolitan's cross (Pl. 32 A and B), it immediately becomes apparent that both are the work of the same master — Baldini. It may be noted, too, that in both the cross and the pax there are what amount to parallel performances. In the former, Baldini worked after the designs of Pollaiuolo and Finiguerra; in the latter he copied (and slightly modified) a pax that had already been made by Pollaiuolo and Finiguerra. Even the modifications of the Crucifixion composition are significant. The original design was harmoniously planned and open; the Baldini modification is turgid and constricted, and the fine essence of the original is lost. As Vasari so truly observed, and as we shall see more clearly later, Baccio was far from gifted when involved with problems of design.

NOTE

In bringing the subject of nielli to a close, mention should be made of a considerable group of related pieces that were not produced by any of the masters to be met with in the course of this study. Because of their importance, and because they are Florentine and fall within the period with which we are concerned, we cannot completely overlook them.

This group consists of the nielloed book cover bearing the arms of Cardinal Balue, now in the Cleveland Museum of Art, with its companion piece, the back cover in the Alphonse de Rothschild collection (Eugène Dutuit, *Manuel de l'amateur d'estampes, Nielles*, Paris, 1888, Vol. I, Part II, plates following p. 50); the ten niello plaques for a book cover in the British Museum (Arthur M. Hind, *Nielli*, London, 1936, pls. V and VI); the niello pax of the Crucifixion in the Bargello (Hind, *op. cit.*, pl. II в); the plaque of the Madonna and Child Enthroned between Two Angels in the Wallace Collection, London; and various small medallions such as items 19 and 28 in Mr. Hind's catalogue of the nielli in the British Museum.

Events in the life of Cardinal Balue indicate that his book covers may be dated between 1467 and 1469. A similar date may apply to all this group. Their designer would seem to have been a retrograde master following in the footsteps of Fra Filippo and others. The Daniel in the Lion's Den in the British Museum book-cover series, for example, is seemingly a reflection of the Saint Mammes in the National Gallery, London, by an assistant to Fra Filippo. Their engraver, for want of a precise name, may be called the "Master of Cardinal Balue's book covers."

II

INTARSIAS

PART I

REPORT

Finiguerra

On February 21, 1464 (new style), the painter Alesso Baldovinetti noted in his *Ricordi* that he had colored the heads of five figures in two intarsia panels made after the designs of Maso Finiguerra for the Sacristy of Santa Liperata (the Duomo of Florence).

> Giuliano di Nardo dam Majano de' dare addì 21 di Febraio 1463 lire 3, e' qua' denari sono per cinque teste gli cholori a cinque fighure disegniate di mano dit Tommaso Finighuerri, cioè una nostra Donna, uno angniolo, uno santo Zanobi chon dua diachoni dallato, le quali fighure sono nella sagrestia di santa Liperata . . . lire 3.
> · From Alesso Baldovinetti, *Ricordi*, Libro A, carta 3, tergo, as quoted by Ruth Wedgwood Kennedy in *Alesso Baldovinetti* (New Haven, 1938), p. 236.

PART 2

FINIGUERRA

In the preceding Section on Nielli, perhaps one feature of Finiguerra's art stands out above all others — its elusiveness — well camouflaged as it is under the lines and forms of other masters. Actually his whole career was the bland acknowledgment of the fact that he was wanting in original talent. Even in his early years as a niellist, he took for his own the designs of his master Ghiberti and of the painter Fra Filippo

25

Lippi. Later, when he was associated with Pollaiuolo, he added that master's style to his growing bag of tricks. Since this was the true nature of the man, small wonder then that scholars of our day have been at a loss to evaluate his work.

That this was indeed the manner of the artist is also shown by his works in other media: intarsia, drawing, and copperplate engraving. With respect to intarsia, the case is particularly interesting in view of the misunderstandings that have cropped up about it. We may be sure that Maso made the designs for five of the woodwork panels installed in the Sacristy of the Duomo of Florence. Two of them, the Annunciation (Pl. 37) and the Saint Zenobius flanked by two deacons, Saints Eugene and Crescentius (Pls. 34, 35 A, and 40 A), the latter now in the Museo dell'Opera del Duomo, were specifically mentioned by Baldovinetti in his *Ricordi* as being after Maso's designs. It may be noted in passing that the commission for making the Sacristy intarsias, of which these two formed part, had been awarded to the architect-woodworker Giuliano da Maiano in July of 1463. Giuliano had called in others, presumably including Maso, to assist him, and the work was virtually completed by the end of February of 1464.

Curiously enough, modern scholars have in general disregarded the evidence of the *Ricordi*, and have assigned these two panels to Baldovinetti. It would seem, however, that the document in question simply cannot be dismissed. If anyone but Baldovinetti had made such a statement, we might be free to doubt it, if we wished, on the grounds that it was irresponsible hearsay. We cannot, however, give to Baldovinetti works of art which he himself categorically assigned to another.

Actually the problem is readily resolved. Just as we discovered the Finiguerran nielli by finding examples containing decided elements of the styles of other masters, we now use a similar paradoxical approach to show that the *Ricordi* was correct, and that Maso was indeed the intarsias' designer. In this instance, however, a new influence is discernible, for we shall find Baldovinetti now sharing with Pollaiuolo the rôle of determining the nature of Finiguerra's compositions.

Alesso and Maso were certainly old acquaintances. In 1449, when they were both at the beginnings of their careers, Baldovinetti wrote in what was the first entry in his *Ricordi* that he had exchanged a dagger for *uno zolfo di mano di Tommaso Finiguerra tornito a sue spese* (a sulphur [cast of a niello] from the hand of Tommaso Finiguerra, made at his own expense). Ruth Wedgwood Kennedy, in *Alesso Baldovinetti* (New Haven, 1938, pp. 27 f.), has pointed out that this master "was never exclusively associated with painters. Jewelers, enamel-workers, engravers, cabinet-makers, glass-painters and mosaicists were among his closest friends, and he was always in touch with that busy group of craftsmen who carried the Florentine canons of taste into the decorative arts."

So it is not altogether surprising to discover that two of the Sacristy panels are very evidently in Baldovinetti's style. One of them is the Saint Zenobius piece, the

26

design of which Baldovinetti declared to be by Maso. The other is the Presentation in the Temple (Pl. 36), of which there is no ancient record of the designer. My belief is that both were designed by Finiguerra. They are almost a pair, and have the same architectural background of shell-topped niches. Both have strongly Baldovinettian characteristics. Take, for example, the panel depicting Saint Zenobius and compare the deacon at his right (Pl. 35 A) with Saint Lawrence (Pl. 35 B) in Baldovinetti's Cafaggiolo altarpiece in the Uffizi. Is there not a more than casual resemblance between the two? As for the Presentation panel, Mrs. Kennedy has observed (*op. cit.*, p. 121) that "the Virgin rushing into the shrine to the left is almost a comic recollection of the Gabriel of S. Giorgio, the baby is a curiously reversed version of the Louvre Christ Child, and the other saints are travesties of the Cafaggiolo martyrs." Incidentally, all the paintings referred to in this passage are by Baldovinetti. It is these very resemblances to Baldovinetti that convince me that the Presentation in the Temple, like its companion Zenobius panel, is also a work by Maso.

Three other intarsia panels in the Sacristy may also be related to Finiguerra: the Annunciation (Pl. 37) and the two panels of the prophets Amos and Isaiah (Pls. 38 and 39 B). The two prophets flank the Annunciation, forming a continuous wainscotting that extends across the wall opposite the entrance to the room. All three panels show the same style; they have similar architectural backgrounds — severely Roman in character, in contrast to the more linear, Florentine ornament of the Saint Zenobius and the Presentation in the Temple panels. The three were surely designed by the same master, and, as already noted, we have Baldovinetti's word for it that the central Annunciation group was the work of Finiguerra.

Yet in style these panels differ greatly from the Zenobius and the Presentation: they are far more powerful compositions, and the figures are drawn with greater verve and assurance. Nor do we have to look long to find behind them the almost imperceptibly veiled presence of Antonio Pollaiuolo. Indeed, point by point we are drawn to the conclusion that another instance of design collaboration would seem to be indicated. The Roman style of the architectural background, for instance, is more that of Pollaiuolo than of Finiguerra. The Virgin of the Annunciation panel may be compared with the Magdalen of the Metropolitan's cross, a work on which Finiguerra had collaborated with Pollaiuolo. And the two panels of Isaiah and Amos have a force and dignity that no artist then at work — save Pollaiuolo — would likely have given them. For purposes of comparison, a drawing of a man (Pl. 39 A) attributed by Bernard Berenson to Antonio Pollaiuolo, and considered by Sergio Ortolani to be a copy of one of Pollaiuolo's drawings, is placed beside the Isaiah. In passing it may be noted that recently the two prophets were attributed to Pollaiuolo for the first time; Dr. Ortolani makes the ascription, adding a question mark (*Il Pollaiuolo*, pp. 193 f., pls. 30 and 31).

Surely, then, Pollaiuolo was the silent partner in this enterprise, for Maso seems to have taken the designs of his associate with but little change when he developed his compositions for the Sacristy walls. Yet, as we might by now expect from our study of Maso's works, there was just enough significant alteration to support the theory that they worked together. It is hardly without significance that the head of a Deacon (in the style of Baldovinetti) and the head of the prophet Amos (in the style of Pollaiuolo) were both drawn feature for feature in the same manner (Pl. 40 A and B). Hence, following the lead of Baldovinetti in his *Ricordi*, we can do no less than credit Maso with the design of the Annunciation; we go beyond Baldovinetti in also assigning to Maso the designs for the two flanking prophets. At the same time we must also credit Finiguerra and Pollaiuolo with another of their collaborative undertakings, with Maso surely not playing the lesser rôle as far as official recognition was concerned. Such a state of affairs would, indeed, lead us to believe that in public esteem Finiguerra was then not the less renowned of the two masters.

III

DRAWINGS

REPORTS

Finiguerra

1. In a manuscript, the Zibaldone Quaresimale, a Lenten notebook begun in 1459, Giovanni Rucellai, the great Florentine merchant, mentioned both the goldsmith Maso Finiguerra and Antonio Pollaiuolo as master draughtsmen working for the Casa Rucellai.

> Memoria che noi abbiamo in casa nostra più cose di scolture e di pitture e di tarsia a rimessi di mano de' migliori maestri che siano stati da buono tempo in qua non tanto in Firenze ma in Italia, i nomi de' quali sono questi, cioè:
>
> . . . .
>
> Antonio d'Iacopo del Polaiuolo maestro di disegno;
> Maso Finiguerra orafo maestro di disegno; . . .
> · From G. Marcotti, *Un Mercante fiorentino e la sua famiglia nel secolo XV* (Florence, 1881), pp. 67 f.

2. In his *Ricordi*, Baldovinetti stated in February of 1464 that Maso Finiguerra had drawn the designs for two of the intarsia panels in the Sacristy of the Florentine Duomo. (For the exact citation of this document see Section II, Part 1.)

3. Vasari recorded that Finiguerra drew well and in abundance, and he added that in his portfolio were many drawings by Maso of figures, both draped and nude, and scenes done in water color. Vasari also noted that in competition with Maso, "Antonio [Pollaiuolo] made several compositions in which he equaled him in diligence, and surpassed him in drawing."

> Costui [Finiguerra] disegnò benissimo, e assai, e nel libro nostro v'è di molte carte di vestiti, ignudi, & di storie disegnate daquerello. A concorrenza di costui fece Antonio alcune istorie dove lo paragonò nella diligenzia; & superollo nel disegno.
> · From Vasari, *Vite* (2nd ed.; Florence, 1568), Seconda Parte, *Vita d'Antonio, & Piero Pollaiuoli*, p. 466.

PART 2

FINIGUERRA

As a practicing goldsmith Maso naturally knew how to make drawings. That he had a reputation as a draughtsman is apparent from the writings of two of his contemporaries, Giovanni Rucellai and Alesso Baldovinetti. The former wrote in his Zibaldone Quaresimale, a notebook commenced in 1459, that the goldsmith Maso Finiguerra, a *maestro di disegno* (master draughtsman), had been working for the Casa Rucellai. The latter declared in his *Ricordi* that Maso supplied designs for intarsia panels in the Sacristy of the Florentine Duomo. In 1568, more than a century later, Vasari recorded that Finiguerra "always drew well and in abundance," and he added that in his portfolio were "many drawings by Maso of figures, both draped and nude, and scenes done in water color." Vasari also stated that Pollaiuolo was Finiguerra's superior in draughtsmanship.

Curiously enough, however, Maso has the sad distinction of being a draughtsman without drawings. None of the many drawings that must have come from his hand has in modern times been definitely attributed to him. He is barely mentioned in Bernard Berenson's classic work on the subject, *The Drawings of the Florentine Painters* (Chicago, 1938, Vol. I, p. 29). Yet "there exists," Mr. Berenson observes, "scattered among various collections, a fairly large number of drawings by a feeble draughtsman whose manner proves him to have been a close follower of the young Antonio Pollaiuolo, although signs of his having been influenced by Baldovinetti are not wanting. There has of late been a tendency to identify this childish craftsman with Maso Finiguerra." That and a footnote suffice for Maso.

In our effort to revive this master's artistic career, we need not critically examine every minor scrap of paper on which he may or may not have set down his line. We confine our attention to that strange and extraordinary monument in the history of Italian drawing known as the Florentine Picture-Chronicle, a series of drawings formerly attributed to Maso, but in recent years no longer believed to be his work. Since this chronicle occupies a central place in our study, we begin with its description and history.

The Florentine Picture-Chronicle is a world history, organized according to the usual medieval plan for such compendia. With the exception of occasional inscriptions added by the draughtsman, there is no text. The work is composed of fifty-five folio sheets, the dimensions of which are about nine by thirteen inches (22.4–23.3 × 31.8–32.7 cm.). As all but three of these have drawings on both sides, there is a total of one hundred and seven drawings. These were drawn in pen with brown ink, have a brown wash, and show traces of under-drawing in black chalk.

As a "chronicle," the book is unfinished; it was evidently planned to be in six parts — the standard arrangement of such works — and there are only five; the sixth part, that which would begin with the Birth of Christ, was left undrawn. The first four folios, those dealing with the Creation, long ago were removed from the book. They are lost.

The Chronicle was first published by the British Museum's Keeper of Prints and Drawings, Sidney Colvin (*A Florentine Picture-Chronicle*, London, 1898). In a splendidly compiled volume with facsimile reproductions of the whole Chronicle (except for four leaves not acquired by the Museum until 1900), Colvin developed the theory that the draughtsman was Maso Finiguerra. Although critics of Italian art at first accepted this attribution, during the course of years Colvin has been left with fewer and fewer supporters. Brilliant though his intuition was, he lacked the forceful arguments to sustain it.

So it is that the whole theory came to be discarded. In the Introduction to his *Early Italian Engraving* (London, 1938), Arthur M. Hind admitted the idea's attractiveness and regretted that it could not be accepted. Finally in 1950, in the British Museum catalogue *Italian Drawings* (no. 274, p. 175), A. E. Popham and Philip Pouncey listed the Chronicle as the work of an anonymous master, "Florentine, about 1460–1470." They dismissed Finiguerra regretfully, for they noted that "It must, in fairness to Colvin, be pointed out that his attribution, while emphatically not proved, cannot, in the present state of our knowledge, be satisfactorily disproved."

So much for the reverse side of the medal. We now re-examine the question in the light of what we have discovered about Maso Finiguerra in our study of nielli and intarsias. If the Chronicle drawings are indeed by him, they should fit into the pattern of his work as we are coming to know it. With this in mind, we can apply certain tests to them. If the Chronicle drawings should meet these tests, which as we shall see are surely too definitive in their character to be applicable to any other master, they must then be by Maso. The tests which I propose are as follows:

First, we have seen that during his early career Finiguerra was a member of the Ghiberti workshop, and that a number of his nielli reflect the influence of his great master. One way, therefore, of indicating the Chronicle to be by Maso would be to demonstrate that drawings in it are based on Ghibertian prototypes.

Second, as various nielli by Maso reveal an indebtedness to Fra Filippo Lippi, another way of showing that Maso was the author of the Chronicle would be to cite occasions in which this same Filippesque manner is to be observed in the Chronicle.

Third, since Finiguerra collaborated with Pollaiuolo both in producing nielli and in designing the Sacristy intarsias, still another way of indicating that the

33

Chronicle was by Maso would be to demonstrate that the draughtsman in question also showed decidedly Pollaiuolan characteristics.

Fourth, since Maso has been shown to have designed panels for the Sacristy intarsias, we should also look for a connection between these works and the Chronicle drawings.

Fifth, evidence connecting the Chronicle with copperplate engravings would give further support to the attribution. Maso's name has always been coupled with the origin of print making in Florence, a matter discussed later on in this work. Various scholars have cited numerous instances in which minor details from Chronicle compositions appear in early prints. As we shall see in Part 4 of the next Section there are indeed some prints which are clearly adaptations from Chronicle designs. Nevertheless, conclusive evidence has yet to be brought to light to prove that any engravings were actually designed by the Chronicle's draughtsman. Such evidence, therefore, should also be sought after.

Sixth, and last, since our findings reveal that a whole group of nielli was engraved by Finiguerra, we should expect to find the style of engraving used for the nielli to be closely reflected in the Chronicle drawings.

Now to the tests themselves, beginning with the first, the Ghiberti test. On the opening leaf of the Picture-Chronicle as it is preserved, Adam is shown with a pick in his hand (Pl. 41 B). Can there be any doubt that this drawing depends to a considerable extent upon Ghiberti's Samson (Pl. 41 A) from the enframement of the Baptistry "Gates of Paradise"? Note, for instance, the resemblance of the two torsos. Adam's figure follows the Ghiberti model exactly as to anatomical structure, and is treated in the same soft, generalized manner. There is even a suggestion of similarity in the heads of the two figures and in the placing of the legs.

In a like manner, the Chronicle's prophet Samuel (Pl. 42 B) is based on one of Ghiberti's prophets (Pl. 42 A). Here the similarity is both general and specific. There is the same three-quarters profile pose, and the same attitude of reading: the prophet in bronze pointing to a scroll held in his left hand, Samuel pointing in the same manner to a book. Under the right elbows of both prophets, heavy folds of drapery are caught up and held against the body; indeed, the whole system of treating the drapery is much the same. Even the pose of the feet is similar.

Consider one more pair of single figures (Pl. 43 A and B), in this instance chosen not to show a specific appropriation of a Ghiberti design, but to reveal how one of the characteristic Chronicle illustrations is fully in the spirit of Ghiberti. The bronze figure is from the relief of the Fall of Jericho, and represents Joshua commanding his troops. The Chronicle drawing shows Minos as king and lawgiver. In both figures a similar concern is shown for the effect of small ornament, as on crown, helmet, armor, and other apparel. Such a concern is typical of the goldsmith, and, of course, Ghiberti and Finiguerra were masters of that art. We also note that both Joshua and

34

Minos are represented as bearded, patriarchal, and almost Semitic in countenance. It may be added that Minos exemplifies a whole group of characters in the Chronicle who in figure, face, or costume derive more or less closely from Ghibertian prototypes. May we not then conclude that the Baptistry doors constituted a kind of sculptural thesaurus for the master of the Chronicle? There seems to be something of Ghiberti on almost every page.

One final comparison should suffice to establish our point beyond any doubt. In one of the Baptistry reliefs Moses is shown on Mount Sinai, receiving from God the Tables of the Law (Pl. 44 B); and in the Chronicle the same composition has been used with little alteration (Pl. 44 A). The resemblance is clear. The differences are equally clear, for they signify the contrasting statures of the two masters. Ghiberti's portrayal is a thing of mighty sweep and power. In the Chronicle drawing the action has been slowed down to a pedestrian level.

The second test is the comparison of Chronicle drawings with Finiguerra's nielli in the style of Fra Filippo Lippi. For this we have as a standard the nielloed plaque of the Agony in the Garden (Pl. 45 A), a panel which, as we have seen, was designed by Finiguerra in a Filippesque manner (Section I, Part 4). When we compare it with the drawing of the Death of Aeschylus (Pl. 45 B), we find that the two have much in common. The rather clumsily drawn figures are placed similarly against their backgrounds; and the backgrounds themselves are much alike. In each case we find pygmy trees in the middle distance that contrast sharply with their larger brethren. There is even a similar way of representing the foliage of these strange trees.

Third, we come to the Pollaiuolo test, for which our standard is the engraving of the Battle of the Naked Men (Pl. 52), a self-identifying work, containing as it does — within a cartouche suspended from a branch at one side of the print — the legend: OPUS ANTONII POLLAIOLI FLORENTTINI. Our test turns out to be a telling one for, as we shall presently see when we come to discuss engravings, it throws new light not only on the Chronicle but on this famous print itself.

On the first page of the Chronicle two scenes are represented. The upper one tells the story of Adam and Eve, and the Adam from this scene (Pl. 41 B) has already been connected with the style of Ghiberti. In the lower one (Pl. 46 B; reversed for comparison), Cain is about to strike the cringing body of his brother with an upraised club. He stands on his right foot, his left leg swung behind him. The composition seems to be borrowed directly from the Battle of the Naked Men, in which the second warrior from the left (Pl. 46 A) holds a similar position, only in reverse.

In another Chronicle drawing, that of Hermes Trismegistus, a nude figure is represented which also may be compared with a warrior from the famous Battle print (Pl. 47 A and B). Here the comparison leaves room for no uncertainty. Detail for detail, the Chronicle drawing follows the figure of the engraving's central warrior, who is holding a chain, his back to us. In both drawing and engraving the out-

35

lines of the legs are virtually identical. Even the tiny details of the drawing betray its origin. For example, Pollaiuolo has treated a knot of muscles at the base of the spine in what seems to be a curious distortion of human anatomy; and the Chronicle draughtsman has done his unsuccessful best to repeat this idiosyncrasy. Although many other of the drawings are also Pollaiuolan in form, the Cain and Trismegistus surely present clinching evidence of the dependence of the draughtsman on the works of Pollaiuolo.

The fourth test concerns intarsia; and in this instance Sidney Colvin has already partially uncovered the evidence for us (*Florentine Picture-Chronicle*, pl. 90 and text and cuts facing that plate) in comparing the prophet Isaiah (Pl. 50 B), one of the intarsia panels in the Sacristy of the Duomo, with the Chronicle's prophet Hosea (Pl. 50 c). From our standpoint, however, his conclusions were defective. He correctly observed that the general posture, the turn of the bearded head, and the oratorical pose of the right hand were the same in both figures. He did not, however, note that the Isaiah was a design that Maso had adapted with but little alteration from the work of his associate, Pollaiuolo. Viewed in this light, the confrontation takes on its real meaning. In drawing the Hosea, the Chronicle draughtsman was simply making use of a design by Pollaiuolo which Finiguerra had already used for the Sacristy panel. Yet this does not entirely explain the genesis of the Chronicle drawing, for there is a further influence discernible, that of another of Ghiberti's prophets (Pl. 50 A), from which the Chronicle draughtsman has taken his system of draping the figure. So it is that the Hosea is both a symbol and a synthesis, based as it is on the designs of these two great renaissance masters.

Our fifth test concerns copperplate engraving. To show that the author of the Chronicle was also a print-designer of first rank, we offer two details from the engraving of the Triumph of Love, one of the six panels forming the series known as the Vienna Triumphs of Petrarch. The figure of Talthybius (Pl. 48 A) from the Chronicle drawing of Palamedes and Talthybius may be compared with the personage (Pl. 48 B) walking at the side of Love's triumphal chariot. And the Helen (Pl. 49 A) from the Chronicle drawing of Paris and Helen may also be compared with the richly gowned lady (Pl. 49 B) who follows Love's chariot and, like Helen, is escorted by a cavalier. In both instances the resemblance is, I think, undeniable. Both are very similar, yet I am convinced that neither the drawing nor the engraving is a copy of the other, for each has its own independence. It is as if each found a common origin in the hand of a draughtsman who lacked the originality to invent new figures, and so reinvested his old figures in a new composition.

Sixth, and last, is the niello test. For this we are concerned not with stylistic connections, but with a comparison of Finiguerra's technique as an engraver of nielli with the technique revealed by the draughtsman of the Chronicle. For such an experiment we use two figures that are quite similar in design: one of the maidens

36

from the niello print of the Arming of Hector (Pl. 51 A), engraved by Finiguerra after a design made in collaboration with Pollaiuolo, and the Amazon from the Chronicle drawing of Theseus and the Amazon (Pl. 51 B), a work that also shows the impact of Pollaiuolo's art.

Even allowing the differences of medium, we find that technically they have everything in common. In each case the line is alert, fluid, yet definite, as in the lower edges of both upper garments. Shading is incidental in both instances, and it has the form of short, sketchy parallel lines, emphasized by an occasional pocket of solid black shadow. We may therefore conclude that technically the engraver of the nielli and the Chronicle draughtsman worked in the same identical styles.

Our evidence is now complete. Since without exception in all six tests — five of them stylistic, the sixth, and not least significant, technical — the conclusions are favorable to the idea that Finiguerra was the designer of the Chronicle, we must, I believe, conclude that this famous work is indeed by him and by no one else. To repeat Colvin's gallant summary of the problem: "Aut Finiguerra, aut diabolus!"

Now that we may feel sure that the Chronicle is the work of Maso, we at once view it in sharper focus. Especially is this so with respect to chronology. Since we know that Maso died in August of 1464 — he was buried on the twenty-fourth of the month — his Chronicle is obviously of a prior date. On the evidence of one of the drawings included, the Chronicle seems to have been done in the final year of his life. This drawing is the prophet Hosea (Pl. 50 c), which as we have seen is based on the prophet Isaiah (Pl. 50 b), one of the intarsia panels in the Sacristy of the Duomo that had been ordered in July of 1463 and that seems to have been almost completed by February of 1464 (Section II, Part 2). At the very earliest, therefore, the Hosea could not have been drawn before the second half of 1463.

Evidence for the latest possible dating of the Chronicle is the fact that it was left unfinished. Is it not reasonable to conclude that death, which came to Maso in August of 1464, stayed his hand before he could complete his task? In view of all these facts and surmises, we can, I believe, accept the first half of 1464 as the probable time for the creation of the Chronicle. And a most significant date this is. As we shall see, it enables us to indicate the correct chronological position of the engravings of the Battle of the Naked Men and of the Vienna Triumphs of Petrarch. More about these, however, when in the following Section we consider in detail the vast and confused problem of the beginnings of Florentine engraving.

IV

COPPERPLATE ENGRAVINGS

DOCUMENTS AND REPORTS

Finiguerra

REPORTS

1. Vasari stated that "the beginning of print engraving then came from the Florentine Maso Finiguerra, about the year of our salvation 1460." He described how Maso began by making sulphur casts of niello plaques, and how prints were made on paper from these plaques. This procedure, according to Vasari, led to the making of copperplate prints.

> Il principio dunque dell'intagliare le stampe venne da Maso finiguerra fiorentino, circa gl'anni di nostra salute 1460, perche costui tutte le cose, che intagliò in argento, per empierle di Niello, le improntò con terra: & gittatovi sopra solfo liquifatto, vennero improntate, e ripiene di fumo, onde à olio mostravano il medesimo, che l'argento. Et cio fece ancora con charta humida, & con la medesima tinta aggravandovi sopra con un rullo tondo, ma piano per tutto. Il che non solo le faceva apparire stampate ma venivano come disegnate di penna.
> • From Vasari, *Vite* (2nd ed.; Florence, 1568), Terza Parte, Primo Volume, *Vita di Marcantonio Bolognese*, p. 294.

2. According to Vasari, the goldsmith Maso Finiguerra "had an extraordinary fame, and deservedly, since there had never been any master of engraving or niello who could make so great a number of figures as he could, whether in small or large spaces . . ." (For the exact citation of this document see Section I, Part 1.)

3. Vasari also wrote that from Maso's engraving of niello plaques are "derived the copper plates from which we see today so many impressions, throughout all Italy, of both Italian and German origin. Just as impressions in clay were taken from silver plaques before they were filled with niello, and casts pulled from them in sulphur, in the same manner printers found out the method of striking off the sheets from the copper plates with the press, as we have seen printing done in our days."

41

Da questo intaglio di bulino son derivate le stampe di rame; onde tante carte, e
Italiane, e Tedesche veggiamo hoggi per tutta Italia, che si come negli argenti
s'improntava, anzi che fussero ripieni di niello, di terra, & si buttava di zolfo, cosi
gli Stampatori trovarono il modo del fare le carte su le Stampe di rame col torculo,
come hoggi habbiam veduto da essi imprimersi.
· From Vasari, *Vite* (2nd ed.; Florence, 1568), Prima Parte, Della Pittura, Cap. xxxiii,
Del Niello, p. 64.

Pollaiuolo

REPORT

Vasari noted that Pollaiuolo, who was the first to demonstrate the method
of searching out the muscles in human anatomy, engraved on copper "a battle of
nude figures all girt round with a chain; and (after making this print) made other
engravings, with much better workmanship than had been shown by any other
(master who had lived before him)."

Egli s'intese degli ignudi piu modernamente, che fatto non havevano gl'altri maestri
inanzi a lui, & scorticò molti huomini, per vedere la notomia lor sotto. Et fu primo
a mostrare il modo di cercar' i muscoli, che havessero forma, & ordine nelle figure;
& di quegli tutti, cinti d'una catena intagliò in rame una battaglia, e (dopo quella)
fece altre stampe [di sua mano], con molto migliore intaglio, che non havevano fatto
gl'altri (maestri, ch'erano stati innanzi a lui).
· From Vasari, *Vite* (2nd ed.; Florence, 1568), Seconda Parte, *Vita d'Antonio, & Piero
Pollaiuoli*, p. 463. The words in parentheses did not appear in the 1550 edition; those
in brackets appeared only in the 1550 edition.

Baldini

REPORT

In his description of the beginnings of engraving in Florence, Vasari declared
that Finiguerra was followed by Baccio Baldini, a Florentine goldsmith who, since
he lacked skill as a draughtsman, worked after the designs of Sandro Botticelli.

Fu seguitato costui [Finiguerra] da Baccio Baldini orefice fiorentino, il quale non
havendo molto disegno, tutto quello, che fece, fu con invenzione, e disegno di Sandro
Botticello.
· From Vasari, *Vite* (2nd ed.; Florence, 1568), Terza Parte, Primo Volume, *Vita di
Marcantonio Bolognese*, p. 295.

Botticelli

1. Vasari reported that the youthful Botticelli was placed by his father in the shop of the goldsmith Botticello. When the lad showed a talent for painting, he was subsequently placed with Fra Filippo Lippi.

> . . . il padre . . . lo pose a lo orefice con un suo compare chiamato Botticello, assai competente maestro all'ora in quell'arte. Era in quella età una dimestichezza grandissima, & quasi che una continova pratica tra gli orefici, & i pittori; per la quale Sandro, che era destra persona, e si era volto tutto al disegno; invaghitosi della pittura, si dispose volgersi a quella. Per il che aprendo liberamente l'animo suo al padre, da lui, che conobbe la inchinazione di quel cervello, fu condotto a fra Filippo del Carmine eccelentissimo pittore all'ora, & acconcio seco a imparare, come Sandro stesso desiderava. Datosi dunque tutto a quell'arte, seguitò & imitò si fattamente il maestro suo, che fra Filippo gli pose amore: & insegnolli di maniera che e' pervenne tosto ad un grado, che nessuno lo harebbe stimato.
> ·From Vasari, *Vite* (2nd ed.; Florence, 1568), Terza Parte, Primo Volume, *Vita di Sandro Botticello*, pp. 470 f.

2. Vasari also wrote that Sandro Botticelli made illustrations for Dante's *Inferno*, as well as making many other designs used for copperplate engravings.

> . . . dove, per essere persona sofistica [Botticelli] comentò una parte di Dante: & figurò lo inferno, & lo mise in Stampa dietro alquale consumò di molto tempo, perilche non lavorando fu cagione d'infiniti disordini alla vita sua. Mise in stampa ancora, molte cose sue di disegni che egli aveva fatti ma in cattiva maniera perche l'intaglio era mal fatto onde il meglio, che si vegga di sua mano è il trionfo della fede, di fra Girolamo Savonarola da Ferrara.
> ·From Vasari, *Vite* (2nd ed.; Florence, 1568), Seconda Parte, *Vita di Sandro Botticello*, pp. 472 f.

Botticelli and Rosselli

In 1528, three years after the death of Alessandro Rosselli, an inventory was made of the contents of his shop. As a son of the cartographer and engraver Francesco Rosselli, who died before 1513, Alessandro had inherited his father's stock in trade. Following is the section of the inventory which lists the engraved metal plates that were part of the Rosselli stock. As will be shown in Section IV, Part 6, a number of these entries describe plates engraved by Francesco Rosselli after the designs of Sandro Botticelli.

(31) 1ª forma de l'appamondo grande nuovo, lavor da ogni banda, di rame.
(32) 1ª forma di lonbardia, in dua fogli chomuni, di rame.
(33) 1ª charta da navichare di dua fogli chomuni, in dua pezi.
(34) 1º cienacholo, da l'altra banda 1ª nostra donna.
(35) 1º appamondo, da l'altra banda 1ª italia d'un foglio reale.
(36) 1º rosaio di fogli reali.
(37) 1º diluvio di foglio reale chol tenpio di salamone.
(38) 1ª morte d'ugolia, da altra banda da storia di muisè, inn un foglio reale.
(39) 1º diluvio d'un foglio reale, e una natività.
(40) 1º giudizo d'un foglio reale, e 'l monte di piatà.
(41) 1ª charta da navichare di 4 fogli chomuni in 2 pezi.
(42) 1º tenpio di pilato, chon meza inchoronazione di nostra donna di 2 fogli reali.
(43) 1ª asensione di 6 (corrected from 4) fogli reali inn un pezo.
(44) 1ª ungheria dopia d'un foglio reale.
(45) 1º appamondo picholo d'u'foglio chomune.
(46) 1ª charta da navichare d'un foglio chomune in tuta.
(47) 1ª francia chon parte di gostantinopoli, in mezo foglio chomune.
(48) 1ª stanpa della palla pichola, d'un foglio chomune.
(49) 1ª form[a] di fregio d'otone, d'un foglio chomune.
(50) 1ª forma di fregi di fogli chomuni, dopia.
(51) 1º sangirgio in dua fogli reali.
(52) 1ª isola di chandia di dua fogli mezani in tutto.
(53) 1ª forma di santori in foglio chomune.
(54) 1ª chonsizione di san pagolo, in foglio reale.
(55) 1ª forma della pala de l'appamondo grande, in sei fogli reali.
(56) 1ª forma da cenboli, in foglio chomune.
(57) 1ª roma in tre pezi in 12 fogli reali.
(58) 1ª italia grande in sei pezi.
(59) 1ª india in 2 pezi, di dua fogli reali.
(60) 1º gostantinopoli in 6 pezi.
(61) 1º appamondo a mantelino, 2 fogli reali in tutto.
(62) 1ª charta grande da navichare, in 4 pezi, d'otto fogli reali.
(63) 1º firenze di sei fogli reali.
(64) 1º appamondo grande in 3 pezi di 12 fogli mezani.
(65) 1º appamondo grande in 9 pezi in 16 fogli chomuni.
(66) 1º grocifisso di foglio chomune.
(67) 1º grocifisso di mezo foglio chomune.
(68) 1º grocifisso di mezo foglio chomune.
(69) 1º san gristofano, 1ª nostra donna, di mezo foglio chomune.
(70) 1ª stanpa di mezo foglio chomune di più santi.
(71) 17 pezi di sobile e profeti, dopie.
(72) 1º giuocho del trionfo del petrarcha in 3 pezi.

(73) 1° giuocho di pianeti chon loro fregi, in 4 pezi.

(74) 1ᵃ santa maria madalena di ½ foglio chomune.

(75) 10 forme di rosai dopi, stanpe di ½ foglio chomune.

(76) 2 teste di dio padre pichole inn otavo foglio.

(77) 1ᵃ vergine maria pichola d'otavo foglio.

(78) 1° grocifisso d'otone d'otavo fogli chon altro.

(79) 1° angnelo rafaelo di stangno di quarto foglio.

Pesorno tutte le sopra dette forme di rame e otone e stangno ll. 475.

· Archivio di Stato, Florence. Magistrato dei Pupilli avanti il Principato, file no. 190, entitled "Filze e inventari di Firenze dall'anno 1526 al 1529," no. 52.

PART 2

POLLAIUOLO

NOTE: In this Part, and frequently thereafter, references will be made to engravings in Arthur M. Hind's *Early Italian Engraving* (Part I, Vol. I, and Part II, Vol. V). We give only the author's name and pertinent entry numbers in these references, omitting the title. References below to engravings in Max Lehrs's *Geschichte und kritischer Katalog des deutschen . . . Kupferstichs im XV Jahrhundert* (Vols. I and IV) are similarly simplified.

In the preceding Section we have seen that two of the drawings in Finiguerra's Picture-Chronicle were adaptations of figures found in Pollaiuolo's engraving of the Battle of the Naked Men (Pl. 52; Hind, D.I.1). It follows then that since Maso died in the summer of 1464 the engraving must have been done previously. Although it has been generally accepted as a work of about 1470, or even later, it would now appear to have been made early in Pollaiuolo's career.

Since in style of engraving there is no other print remotely like it, we may presume that it was Pollaiuolo's only venture as engraver of prints. Yet simply from the standpoint of technique it is one of the most remarkable of all Italian prints. The engraver has partially followed the canons of the contemporary fine-manner engraving, as in his use of a heavy outline for the figures, in accordance with a convention first developed for the making of nielli. For the rest, innovator that he was, he proceeded on his own, developing a technique which prefigures that of the broad manner. The very degree to which Pollaiuolo's engraved line resembles that of the later broad-manner engravings by Rosselli is the degree to which he is responsible for the development of that technique.

From the standpoint of composition also, the print would seem to be of an early date. In support of this we have the two series of the Planets, to which closely approximative dates may be given. Of the two series, which will be discussed more fully later in this Section, the second is a variant of the first. A calendar with directions for finding the day on which Easter falls, beginning with the year 1465, forms part of the second series, which must therefore have been made during 1464 or early in 1465. The original series is obviously earlier; my guess is about 1461–1462, a time indicated by related engravings that we shall consider in subsequent Parts of this Section. A detail from Mars, one of the Planets in the original series, shows a group of men in violent movement (Pl. 57) — a combat similar in general conception to that of the great Battle engraving. Clearly, therefore, on the evidence of the Planets, this sort of design was being produced in Florence in the early 1460s.

Still other evidence may be cited in favor of an early dating for the Battle engraving. There is a small panel of Hercules and the Hydra, belonging to the Uffizi (and now, unfortunately, listed among the war missing), which is certainly the work of Pollaiuolo. Hercules (Pl. 53 B) so resembles the warrior at the extreme left of the Battle engraving (Pl. 53 A) that it seems conclusive that painting and print were executed at about the same period in Antonio's life.

The question is, then, when was the Hercules panel painted? It has generally been considered to be a reduced version, executed by Pollaiuolo himself about 1470, of a large work he had made with the help of his brother Piero for the Casa Medici in 1460. This painting was part of a series of the Labors of Hercules which no longer exists. In his *Drawings of the Florentine Painters* (Vol. I, p. 19, n. 2), Bernard Berenson was not at all sure that the small Uffizi panel was later than the one made for the Casa Medici, shrewdly pointing out that "artists as a rule do not work from large to small, but *vice versa*." But even though it were a later copy, the design would still remain that of 1460, and the validity of the comparison with the Battle engraving would continue unimpaired.

Since the probabilities are that the engraving was made after the Medici pieces had been completed, it can safely be dated between 1460 and 1464, when the Chronicle was drawn. And since from a compositional standpoint it would seem no later than the Planet Mars in which the battle scene already mentioned occurs, we may further narrow the enclosing years to about 1460–1462.

As we have already discovered, Pollaiuolo was by that time working in collaboration with Finiguerra. Finiguerra as the older of the two, and already distinguished as a niellist, may at first have been the leading figure in this association. Yet even then Pollaiuolo was infinitely the more talented, and not one to be held in check. Is it not therefore possible that this very print of the Battle of the Naked Men may have constituted his proud assertion of superiority over his colleague? It may well be that it was the creation of this engraving that caused Vasari to remark that in

46

competition with Finiguerra, Pollaiuolo "equaled him in diligence, and surpassed him in drawing." To equal the already renowned Maso in diligence would be to equal him as an engraver. And certainly the Battle print equals any engraving believed to be the work of Maso. That Pollaiuolo surpassed Finiguerra in drawing goes without saying. And that he affixed his name to the print in a cartouche, which may originally have been planned to contain the title of the composition, would seem to show that Pollaiuolo turned this print into an advertisement of his own genius.

In view of its importance in the history of Florentine engraving, we should ask what the Battle print really represents. Its meaning has long been a source of speculation. Erwin Panofsky (*Albrecht Dürer*, Princeton, 1948, Vol. II, pp. 95 ff.) has recently connected this print with various works, including a drawing in the British Museum of a Prisoner Led before a Judge and an engraving of Hercules and the Giants (Pl. 54; Hind, D.I.2). Dr. Panofsky holds that they and other compositions represent a cycle of events designed by Pollaiuolo from Roman legend. According to this theory, the British Museum drawing depicts Tullius Hostilius rescinding, at the request of the people, the death sentence against one of the Horatii; the Hercules engraving depicts a battle between the Romans and the Carthaginians; and that of the Battle of the Naked Men gives the story of Titus Manlius Torquatus taking a necklace from a Gallic chieftain.

It would seem that Dr. Panofsky has grouped together at least two objects that on the face of things cannot be so joined. For on the basis of all available evidence, the print of Hercules and the Giants was not designed by Pollaiuolo. True it is that it derives in part from the Battle of the Naked Men. The upper halves of the figures of the two bowmen in the Hercules print are adapted from that of the bowman in the Battle of the Naked Men. The lower halves of the figures of the two warriors with sword and shield similarly find their model in the warrior immediately to the right of the bowman in the Battle print (details, Pl. 55 A and B). And the axman in the Hercules print would also seem to be based on a similar figure in the Battle of the Naked Men. If prototypes for the kneeling warrior and the fallen warrior exist in the work of Pollaiuolo, they are to be found in another source — his painting of Saint Sebastian in London's National Gallery. Within the passageway of a ruined triumphal arch in the painting's background, a battle scene is represented upon a rectangular relief. In this scene are the two figures in question. Since, according to Vasari, the Sebastian panel was completed in 1475, it must have been made nearly fifteen years after the engraving of the Battle of the Naked Men. Are not these various borrowings the determining mark of the copyist and follower?

We can hardly believe that a master of Pollaiuolo's brilliance would be so lacking in invention as to be forced over and over again to imitate himself. In other respects, too, the design of Hercules and the Giants seems unworthy of Pollaiuolo. The composition as a whole lacks the taut, organic unity of the famous Battle print and of

47

other works known to have been designed by him. And from the standpoint of engraving technique, it seems — for reasons outlined in the Note at the end of this Part — to have nothing in common with any of the early Florentine prints.

The engraving of the Battle of the Naked Men must therefore stand on its own as a single, independent creation. Nor can its subject be understood in relation to that of any other print or drawing. While this study is in no sense iconographical, we may now make use of such an approach inasmuch as it helps to establish the print as an independently conceived creation, and to give further evidence in favor of an early dating for it.

In 1460, when Pollaiuolo was working in the Casa Medici, Marsilio Ficino was a member of Cosimo de' Medici's household. The great renaissance scholar and philosopher was about Pollaiuolo's age — he was still in his twenties. Professor Paul Kristeller has pointed out that a letter written by Ficino to Pietro Molino (*Epistolae Marsilii Florentini*, Venice, 1495, Book VII, fol. 138) shows that the humanist was actually one of Pollaiuolo's friends. Curiously enough, in their separate ways they were at that time following similar paths: while Pollaiuolo was decorating the Medici walls with the exploits of Hercules, Ficino was translating Orpheus' *Argonautica*, a Greek poem concerned with the exploits of Jason. Although Ficino's translation was never put into print and his manuscript has been lost, we know from one of his letters to Martinus Uranius (*op. cit.*, Book IX, fol. 180) that sometime between about 1458 and 1462 he completed such an undertaking.

Both the paintings and the translation seem to bear on the history of the engraving in question. The stylistic connection between Pollaiuolo's Hercules painting and the engraving has already been established. A connection of another sort apparently existed between Ficino's translation of the *Argonautica* and the Battle print, for an incident related in the poem, that of the Dragon's Teeth, may be said to be the engraving's subject.

Since the Ficino translation no longer exists, and since the reference to the Dragon's Teeth in Orpheus' *Argonautica* is of a sketchy nature, we look for a fuller description of the event to another, earlier version of the Jason legend, that of the Roman poet Valerius Flaccus. As narrated by Flaccus, Jason at one point during his adventures plowed a field and sowed it with the dragon's teeth, and was at once faced with a harvest of fierce warriors who threatened to turn upon him. At that moment Jason disjoined "the chain and fastening at his helmet's base . . . [and] flung into their midst the helmet which Medea of late had drugged . . ." (tr. by J. M. Mozley). The warriors immediately fell upon each other.

This then, the fratricidal strife between the spawn of the Dragon's Teeth, is the story that Pollaiuolo would seem to have represented in the Battle of the Naked Men. Among the indications favoring such a theory is the sharp distinction made between the rank, weedy background and the barren foreground showing the marks of furrows. Is not this the artist's way of making the contrast between the unplowed and plowed areas of the field? Then there is the struggle itself: complete, savage, insane. The figures are not grouped in armies or factions: each of them, sprung naked from the earth, stands alone, independently bent on slaughter, as if, in the words of Flaccus, he believed his closest neighbor to be Jason. As we look at this print, can any issue to this "battle" be envisaged but general annihilation? If Pollaiuolo's Battle print is not an illustration of the story of the Dragon's Teeth, could one be imagined depicting it more effectively?

It would seem likely that Pollaiuolo got his idea for the subject of the print from conversations with Ficino. On the other hand, although it is doubtful whether Pollaiuolo could read Latin, the Jason story was not an unfamiliar one to the Florentines. In addition to the versions by Valerius Flaccus and the author of the *Argonautica*, there were then in circulation the Greek poem by Apollonius Rhodius (the original of all later versions of the Jason story) and other accounts of the legend by Apollodorus, Ovid, Hyginus, and Boccaccio. In general these versions give a similar description of the incident of the Dragon's Teeth; they are not, however, completely alike. In the accounts by Apollonius, Apollodorus, Ovid, and Hyginus, Jason throws a stone or stones among the warriors to rouse them to fight among themselves; we have seen that in Flaccus a helmet replaced the stone; in Orpheus' *Argonautica* there is no mention of stone or helmet. It is a fact that none of the authors describes a chain such as the one for which the two central warriors of the Battle print are struggling. This curious addition to the composition may be explained in various ways. It may be that in faulty recollection of the Flaccus version Pollaiuolo substituted the part (the chain) for the whole (the helmet). Or the chain could simply have been a prop with no significance of its own, boldly chosen by the artist to join the composition together.

Strangely enough, in the history of Florentine art prior to the creation of this print there are seemingly no prototypes for the episode of the Dragon's Teeth. But so independent a master as Pollaiuolo needed no well-sanctioned example. He improvised, perhaps along the lines of some of the early German prints then just beginning to be known in Florence. As we shall see in the next Part of this Section, in collaboration with Finiguerra he later adapted the Fight for the Hose, by the Master of the Banderoles (Pl. 66 B), to create an engraving of this subject in the Italian taste. And in this same German print is found a manner of grouping the figures in space that vaguely recalls the composition of the Battle of the Naked Men. It may be, therefore, that the basis for the latter composition was a German work, rather than, as has generally been presumed, some ancient Roman relief.

Be that as it may, Pollaiuolo would seem to have found the story of the Dragon's Teeth intensely to his liking. It was a perfect vehicle for his genius, permitting him to represent a group of heroically formed nudes in the wildest of actions. If, as Mr.

Berenson has observed (*The Florentine Painters of the Renaissance*, New York, 1909, 3d ed., p. 54), he gave these creatures the "power to directly communicate life, to immensely heighten our sense of vitality," it would seem to be the reckless, unreasoning power of a purely physical nature, a power which, among the living, the strongest and most savage of animals most fully possess. Such a scene as that of the Dragon's Teeth, animated by such a dynamism, needed no story to carry it. The story indeed was soon forgotten; Pollaiuolo's triumph as artist over subject matter was complete.

NOTE

Since the engraving of Hercules and the Giants (Pl. 54) is demonstrably not by Pollaiuolo, the question may be asked: who, then, was responsible for it?

When we set out to discover the identity of the engraver — for it is necessary to distinguish between the engraver and the designer of this work — our search immediately takes us outside Florence. We find, strangely enough, that although the composition is Florentine and Pollaiuolan, the rendering of it on the copper plate is North Italian and, specifically, in the style of Mantegna. Mantegnesque is the way in which the legs of the warrior with sword and shield (Pl. 55 B) have been engraved, as we see by comparing this detail with another (Pl. 56 c) from Mantegna's engraving of the Risen Christ between Saint Andrew and Saint Longinus (Hind, 7); so also is the curious manner of representing the foreground as a stratified rock formation strewn with small stones and pebbles, each with its own cast shadow, as seen by comparing the same detail of the Hercules print with a detail (Pl. 56 D) of a Mantegnesque work by Nicoletto Rosex da Modena, Hercules and Antaeus (Hind, 1).

The warrior fallen to his knees in the center of the print of Hercules and the Giants is apparently a stock figure, as well known among the masters close to Pollaiuolo as to those surrounding Mantegna. The engraving of this particular figure, however, again suggests the work of one closely related to the great North Italian master. Also, the head of the warrior with sword and shield at the left of the Hercules and the Giants composition (Pl. 56 A) is extraordinarily like the head of the central personage in the engraving of Soldiers Carrying Trophies (Pl. 56 B; Hind, 15, B) from the series of the Triumphs of Caesar. It may be noted as an indication of a possible date for the Hercules print that the Triumph engraving is placed by Mr. Hind "after 1492" because the painting by Mantegna which served as its model was not completed until that year.

Then there is the evidence — which, however, is not conclusive — relating the Hercules print to the engraved work of Nicoletto Rosex da Modena, one of Mantegna's followers. We know that this busy North Italian engraver, who was active from the end of the fifteenth century, made use of the designs of Mantegna, and that on occasion he copied engravings by Schongauer and Dürer. Mr. Hind has pointed out that there are also traces of certain Florentine influences in his work; in this respect it is of interest to note that in Nicoletto's Mantegnesque print of Vulcan Forging Cupid's Wing (Hind, 2) the tree that looms large in the background is clearly after the tree in Pollaiuolo's Battle of the Naked Men.

Evidence specifically linking the Hercules print with Nicoletto may also be found in this same Vulcan print: in both works the treatment of the foreground, in which the shaley rock is disintegrating into neat geometric patterns, suggests the work of one master. Furthermore, the lettering to be found in the second state of the Hercules engraving (Hind, D.I.2, II) conforms in general to that found in various engravings known to have been made by Nicoletto. Testimony of this sort, I submit, is surely enough to allow us to suggest that he, or someone working closely in his manner, may have been the engraver of the Hercules print.

So much for the engraver. As for the designer, less can be said with any certainty, although we have already seen that he was not Pollaiuolo himself, but was, rather, one who worked in that master's style. Fortunately, two drawings exist which throw some light on this aspect of the problem.

There is a summarily executed drawing in the Biblioteca Reale in Turin (published by John Walker, *Dedalo*, Anno XIII, Vol. I, 1933, pp. 229-237) which with respect to composition is closely akin to the Hercules print. It may have been a preliminary sketch for the engraving; at any event it is clearly Florentine. Then there is an impressive fragment of another Florentine drawing closely related in composition but executed in a different, more finished manner. It is to be found in the Paul J. Sachs collection of the Fogg Art Museum in Cambridge, Massachusetts (B. Berenson, *Drawings of the Florentine Painters*, no. 1898 c), and its subject faithfully corresponds to a detail of the Hercules print. Whether this drawing is by the same author as the Turin example is open to doubt. At least this much is certain: the drawing in the Fogg Museum is not *after* the Hercules engraving, for it is wholly Florentine in character and possesses none of the Mantegnesque elements of the print. It is, of course, possible that it was created to serve as the engraving's model. I feel it more probable, however, that it was conceived as an independent work, and that a North Italian engraver later reproduced it through the medium of printing, just as he might have reproduced a popular work by Dürer or Schongauer.

From the relation of drawing to engraving, we can say that the designer of the Fogg Museum's example was active in Florence during the last quarter of the fifteenth century. He must, however, be classed with the anonymous. It would, indeed, be interesting to know more about this gifted follower of Pollaiuolo, to whom, it seems to me, may also be attributed the famous drawing in the British Museum of the Prisoner Led before a Judge (Berenson, *op. cit.*, no. 1906).

PART 3

FINIGUERRA AND POLLAIUOLO

We discovered earlier in this study that Finiguerra and Pollaiuolo must have worked pretty much as equals in the matter of designing nielli, with Finiguerra seemingly supplying a number of the original ideas to be set down in precise form by Pollaiuolo. The completed designs were then engraved by Finiguerra. Now as we study copperplate prints, we shall find just about the same situation.

When these two masters were working together, copperplate engraving was a new art in Florence. In relating its origins to niello work, Vasari wrote that "the beginning of print engraving then came from the Florentine Maso Finiguerra, about the year of our salvation 1460." Vasari also noted that Maso Finiguerra had "an extraordinary fame, and deservedly, since there had never been any master of engraving or niello who could make so great a number of figures as he could, whether in small or large spaces." Mr. Hind believes, and I concur with him, that when Vasari referred to small spaces he meant nielli, and that when he referred to large spaces he meant coppers. And it would seem to follow that just as the nielli already attributed to Finiguerra as engraver fit the first half of Vasari's description, the prints that will now be attributed to him as engraver fit the second half. With regard to Pollaiuolo, Vasari noted that after that master had made the "battle of nude figures," he "made other engravings, with much better workmanship than had been shown by any other (master who had lived before him)." And again we shall find that our evidence is in general agreement with Vasari's report.

Outstanding among the early Florentine prints are the two series of the Planets, to which we referred in our analysis of the Battle of the Naked Men. We are at this time concerned with the first, the original, series (Hind, A.III.1,a–7,a). Not only are the designs of each of these seven Planets in the style of Pollaiuolo, but they are crowded with figures in the Finiguerra manner, recalling as vividly as do any of the early Florentine engravings the words of Vasari. Hence they would seem to relate to both Pollaiuolo and Finiguerra. Following the sequence already used in the examination of nielli, let us first endeavor to connect them with the style of Antonio Pollaiuolo.

To show that the designs are partly his work, we shall begin with a detail from the Planet Mars (Hind, A.III.3,a), the battle scene (Pl. 57) to which we have already referred. Can it be doubted that this particular scene was from the hand of a consummate master draughtsman? The figure at the right, for instance, with spade in hand; the man in the center, wielding an ax; the soldier with a long spear at the left: each of these is a study in the most delicate sort of balance. The general tenor of the composition recalls that found in the Battle of the Naked Men. Both show a high order of draughtsmanship which — despite the presence of Maso as engraver of the Planet Mars — may, I feel, be traced to one designer, that is, to Pollaiuolo. This, I think, would hold even though the design was actually drawn on the copper plate by Finiguerra.

Let us take another detail, this one from the engraving of the Planet Moon (Pl. 59; Hind, A.III.7,a), in which boys are shown swimming and fishing in a stream. When we compare one of the figures in this scene, the boy at the farthest left (Pl. 58 A), with the niello print of a Seated Nude Youth (Pl. 58 B), we find that the two designs must have derived from the hand of one master. And as we have already seen (Section I, Part 3), the design of the niello may be attributed to Pollaiuolo.

These evidences of the participation of Pollaiuolo are undoubtedly strong. Yet when we observe the designs of the Planets as a whole, we note within each of them a certain basic discordance, the result of a sharp contrast between the representation of the backgrounds and that of the figures. As we have just indicated, the figures themselves show the highest order of draughtsmanship and may be assigned to Pollaiuolo. The backgrounds, which occupy much of the areas of the plates, would seem to be another matter: they are discursive, unorganized, and clumsy. They could hardly be farther from the work of Pollaiuolo, who, as may be seen from his famous panel of Hercules and the Hydra (Pl. 53 B), had already shown himself to be a master of the art of landscape. The parallels of the Planets' backgrounds are rather to be found in the Picture-Chronicle, in which we find that landscape and architectural backgrounds are organized in a similar popular, one might also say "chatty," vein. It is to Finiguerra indeed that the Planet backgrounds are to be attributed.

It is to be observed, on the other hand, that the tiny background figures themselves are finely designed, even the most minute of them. They would not seem to be by Finiguerra as we have come to know him from the more casual Chronicle drawings. On the contrary, they seem to be Pollaiuolo's work. We therefore are led to conclude that after Maso had first sketched in the landscape and architectural backgrounds, both the minor figures of the background and the major ones of the foreground were added on the basis of designs supplied by Pollaiuolo. If such were the case, it would follow that Finiguerra must be credited with the original conception of the Planets. Only in this manner, it seems to me, can the discordances in the Planets' designs be accounted for. So again, if we do not misjudge the evidence, we are led to postulate the existence of this highly organized collaboration in design.

There are, interestingly enough, still other details that throw light on the possible origins of various elements of the Planet compositions. One such detail is found in the Planet Sun (Hind, A.III.4,a), in which various gymnasts are shown disporting themselves (Pl. 60 A). Another, from the Planet Venus (Hind, A.III.5,a), has as its subject an amorous bathing scene (Pl. 60 B). In the analysis of Pollaiuolo's Battle of the Naked Men, we noted the possibility of German influence in the plan of its composition. The same possibility may also apply to the Planets. For, as revealed by comparative illustrations, the two Planet details cited above seem intimately related to a print (Pl. 61) of a Tilting Gallery and a Bathing Scene by the German Master of the Banderoles (Max Lehrs, *Geschichte und kritischer Katalog des deutschen . . . Kupferstichs im XV Jahrhundert*, Vienna, 1921, IV.149.99). If, as seems likely, the German print is the earlier, we would appear to have another instance of a Northern engraving influencing Florentine design at the crucial moment when print making was an infant art in Italy and Italian designers had not as yet developed a self-sustaining tradition.

So far we have considered the Planets with reference to their designers and their designs. That their engraver was also Maso Finiguerra should be self-evident. When from the standpoint of engraving alone we compare the niello print of the Seated Nude Youth (Pl. 58 B) with the detail of the young man from the engraving of the Moon (Pl. 58 A), we discover that they have a common origin. In both are the same strong, fluid outlines that give the designs much of their essential character, and the same curiously flat treatment of the body. It will be remembered that in the Section on Nielli we have already credited Finiguerra with the engraving of the Seated Nude Youth. A similar line of reasoning can only lead us to the same attribution with respect to the Planets.

In addition to the Planets, there are certain individual prints offering further evidence of the Finiguerra-Pollaiuolo collaboration. Two of the most notable are the companion engravings of the Triumph of Bacchus and Ariadne (Hind, A.II.26, left half and right half). It is a matter of record that they have always been dated late in the fifteenth century, and have often been related by various scholars to Botticelli. Although Mr. Hind now classes them as anonymous works of about 1470–1480, it seems fair to say that the aura of Botticelli still clings to them. Yet a correct assessment of the stylistic evidence would surely suggest a far different authorship and dating. The fact is that in style they are intimately related to the Planets. Note, for example, how the figure of a girl with a flail (Pl. 62 A), a Pollaiuoloan detail from the Planet Saturn (Hind, A.III.1,a), compares with the second figure from the right in the left panel of the Triumph of Bacchus and Ariadne (Pl. 63). In both instances there is the same head, with the hair so unusually represented, the same movement of the body, and the same drapery: in short, the same girl.

Other Pollaiuolan details are just as telling. To cite but one, a pig carried on the shoulder of a maiden in the same Triumph print (Pl. 63) is delineated in precisely the style of the swine that are being slaughtered in the engraving of Saturn.

As we might expect, minor elements in the designs of these twin Triumph prints would seem to be by Finiguerra. Surely the vine boughs, which form such a conspicuous feature of the composition, and possibly also the chariot of Bacchus, were his work. In describing the engraving Mr. Hind has noted that "in the design of the vine boughs and clusters the work shows close analogy to a drawing of the *Picture-Chronicle* [of the Drunkenness of Noah]." As indicated by a detail of the Finiguerra drawing (Pl. 62 B), this resemblance indeed seems to be more than an analogy; it is an exact correspondence of style.

It must be concluded, therefore, that Finiguerra worked with Pollaiuolo on the Triumph design; it is even likely, as in the case of the Planets, that he established its broad definitions, putting in the chariot and the vines and leaving the decisive figure delineation to his partner. It is also more than just possible that the general idea of the composition with its troop of women in wind-blown draperies was Maso's, for, as we have already seen in Section I, Part 3, the related maidens in the niello print of the Arming of Hector (Pl. 12 B) would appear to have been borrowed by him and not by Pollaiuolo from an earlier composition of Fra Filippo Lippi. As we shall discover later in this Section, the young Botticelli was working in the same shop with Finiguerra and Pollaiuolo. Is it too much to suggest that this same Filippesque-inspired design for the Triumph of Bacchus and Ariadne was in fact a basis for the composition that Botticelli was to create years later, and far more elegantly, of the Primavera?

There is a whole group of prints that fit into the orbit of the style of the Planets and the Triumph engravings. It seems enough to list some of the characteristic examples. One is the Procession to Calvary and the Crucifixion (Pl. 64; Hind, A.II.8), a print which like the Planets was seemingly designed by Pollaiuolo on the basis of a composition planned by Finiguerra, and then engraved by the latter. Another is the Beheading of a Captive (Pl. 65; Hind, A.II.11). Interestingly enough, this print was many years ago related by Kristeller to a niello print in the Parma Library (*Jahrbuch der Königlichen Preussischen Kunstsammlungen*, XV, 1894, p. 115). That example is now lost, but another one, perhaps issuing from the same plate, is to be found in the Rothschild collection in the Louvre (André Blum, *Les Nielles du quattrocento*, Paris, 1950, no. 35 bis). When the copperplate and the Louvre print are compared, there can be no question of their intimate relationship. The parent design is clearly the niello. Just as Pollaiuolo may be credited with the figures, which are naturally the decisive element in the designs, other details — specifically the candelabra at either side of the copperplate print — seem referable to Finiguerra. Incidentally, the idea for the original design seems to have derived from Donatello's bronze Judith and Holophernes, which about 1460 stood in the courtyard of the Casa Medici.

Among the other prints that may also be classed as the work of our two partners are: the Fight for the Hose (Pl. 66 A; Hind, A.II.5), already described by Mr. Hind as a Florentine adaptation of a German print of the same subject (Pl. 66 B; Lehrs,

55

IV.133.89) by the Master of the Banderoles; the King of the Goats (Pl. 67; Hind, A.II.23), a satire on cuckolds, which may also have been inspired by some German design; and, lastly, the Saint Nicholas, Patron of Sailors (Hind, A.I.62), a design that is possibly of purely Italian origin.

A final word as to the dating of the Pollaiuolo-Finiguerra prints: they all seem to have been made shortly after the time when Pollaiuolo engraved the Battle of the Naked Men. And they must have been made before the summer of 1464, when Finiguerra died. The approximate date of 1461–1462, which partly on the basis of the evidence of the calendar has already been given to the Planet series, thus fits in nicely between the terminal dates, about 1461–1464, for all the Pollaiuolo-Finiguerra prints.

PART 4

BALDINI, I

We have met Baccio Baldini as the engraver of the niello plaques on the Metropolitan's cross and of the Bargello pax of the Crucifixion. We now consider him in more detail as both the designer and engraver of copperplate prints. As we have already noted, he poses a most complicated problem. So elusive has his personality proved to be, that modern criticism has been at a loss to point to even one print and assert that it was his. Baldini has become almost a myth.

Yet in the sixteenth century he was real enough to Giorgio Vasari, who stated that he followed Finiguerra, and was so lacking in ability as a designer that he restricted his activity to engraving and took his designs from Botticelli. That is precisely all we know about him. We do not know when he was born, and even the date of his death is uncertain. We have no more than the record of the burial of a *Baccio orafo* in Florence in 1487, which may or may not refer to him.

Despite this dearth of information, there was a time when scholars, basing their judgments on traditional sources, attributed a number of engravings to his hand. In *Le Peintre Graveur* (1803–1821), Adam Bartsch credited him with the Prophets and the Sibyls, the second series of the Planets, and the illustrations for the Landino edition of Dante's *Divina Commedia* in 1481. In an appendix he attributed a few individual prints to the same artist. Although Bartsch's opinions have long since been discredited, they now appear in the light of our study to have been essentially right.

He would seem to have erred only in attributing too few prints to Baldini and in not fully realizing the nature of his work.

If Vasari was correct in his appraisal of Baldini, we would be concerned with a master who was primarily an engraver. Hence in our approach to him, we reverse the system that has been followed in our study of Finiguerra. We first group together prints which give technical indications of having come from the hand of the same engraver, whom we will endeavor to identify as Baldini. Then, the technical examination completed, we shall, in Part 5 of this Section, review these same prints on the basis of their designs.

In setting out to determine the works he actually engraved, we confine ourselves to a study of those that seemingly are the most significant. By considering them in what would appear to be their approximate chronological order, we hope to outline Baldini's character as an engraver from about 1460, when he presumably first began making prints, until the time of his death, which may have been in 1487.

We shall begin, therefore, by attempting to isolate at least one early example that stands a fair chance of having been engraved by him, and then shall relate it with others possessing similar technical characteristics. Fortunately there is a print, and a very early one at that, bearing an all but obliterated inscription in which the name Baldini may be read. It is the Coronation of the Virgin (Pl. 68; Hind, A.I.12). Mr. Hind feels, with good reason, that it may be Baldini's work, and he states (*Early Italian Engraving*, Vol. I, p. 9) that "if this engraving is actually his, then others in the same manner, such as . . . the *Resurrection with the Table to find Easter*, of 1461 [detail, Pl. 70 A; Hind, A.I.7] may be by his hand." It should be noted here that this Resurrection is the earliest Florentine print to which a definite date — 1460–1461 — can be assigned. With the Coronation and Resurrection prints we may group: the Baptism of Christ (Pl. 69; Hind, A.I.10); the Death and Assumption of the Virgin (Pl. 72; Hind, A.I.11), a work described by Mr. Hind as "probably from the same workshop as the *Resurrection* of 1461"; a Gallant and His Mistress Holding a Crown (Pl. 70 B; Hind, A.IV.19); and Virgil the Sorcerer (detail, Pl. 71 C; Hind, A.I.47).

Without going into a lengthy analysis of their engraving style — the sorry condition of some of these early examples would make such an approach less than decisive — we may nevertheless observe that they have a great deal in common. The same sharp outlines are used throughout to delineate the figures, and the shading is applied indiscriminately in patches, except on heads, hands, and feet, which are generally left unshaded. Such observations, however, are not original with us, although we concur with them; they are from Bartsch's description of what he believed to be Baldini's style of engraving.

Continuing with our list of Baldini's works, we now come to a somewhat later group, including among other items two series closely related in technique: the ten prints of the Vienna Passion (Hind, A.I.25–34) and the six Vienna Triumphs of Petrarch (Hind, A.I.18–23). Their date is securely fixed by the evidence of one in the latter series — the Triumph of Love (Hind, A.I.18) — the design of which, as we have already seen (Section III, Part 2), is clearly contemporaneous with the execution of Finiguerra's Chronicle. In other words, they can be no later than 1464. The connection between the two Vienna series and the earlier Baldini prints would seem to be found in the Virgin and Child Enthroned between Saint Theodore and Saint Catherine (Pl. 74; Hind, A.I.35), a work closely akin in engraving to the Death and Assumption of the Virgin in the earlier group and to prints in the later Passion series.

Shortly thereafter Baldini seems also to have engraved the second Procession to Calvary and the Crucifixion (Hind, A.II.7) and the second series of the Planets (Hind, A.III.1,b–8,b), which according to the testimony of its accompanying calendar was made in 1464 or 1465. As we shall later show, the seeming difference between the second Planets and the Triumphs is due to a different origin of design. Their engraving technique is fundamentally the same, as revealed by comparison of the handling of the ornament of the chariot in the Triumph of Love (Pl. 82) with that of similar details from the Planet Jupiter (Pl. 83). Another relationship, that of a detail of one of the Planets with a detail of the nielloed pax of the Crucifixion in the Bargello (Pl. 84 A and B), is of crucial import for this entire study, for it concerns works in two different media. If we are correct in our theory that Baldini was their engraver, there must be a technical kinship observable in this comparison. As we read the evidence, such kinship does indeed exist.

Baldini's connection with the Planets did not end with the second series, for the borders, or *fregi*, of the first series, which had been engraved by Finiguerra (Section IV, Part 3), would also appear to be Baccio's work. As we shall discover when we examine them as designs, they were made after Maso's death in 1464. In addition to engraving the borders, Baldini seems to have worked minor areas of Finiguerra's plates for the Planets. There are impressions of the Finiguerra-engraved series in the British Museum which indicate that such was the case. Although the reworking evident in these impressions is mostly confined to the shading of certain areas (principally foliage), it is Baldinian in effect and stands out sharply against the delicately controlled surfaces of Finiguerra's creations.

Baldini may be credited with a considerable number of engravings made between about 1465 and 1480, chief among them being the twenty-four Prophets (Hind, C.I.1,a–24,a) and the twelve Sibyls (Hind, C.II.1,a–12,a). Others in this category are the Judgment Hall of Pilate (Pls. 85 and 106; Hind, A.II.9), the Conversion of Paul (detail, Pl. 105 A; Hind, A.II.10), the Virgin and Child Standing before a Throne with Saint Sebastian and Saint Catherine (Pl. 86 A; Hind, A.II.25), and Saint Catherine of Siena (Pl. 87 A; Hind, A.I.66). Although in these engravings Baldini's technique is marked by greater fluency and ease, it still remains characteristically

Baldinian. We may note, for example, the use of the same rather harsh manner of delineating the architectural ornament of the thrones of Pilate (Pl. 85), the Virgin (Pl. 86 A), and the Sibyl Agrippa (Pl. 86 B).

A considerable number of other prints made during this period, including those known as the Otto prints, could be listed as having been engraved by Baldini. Since, however, further evidence would not add materially to our case, we end this technical study by turning to what are believed to be among Baldini's late works, the nineteen illustrations for the Landino edition of 1481 of Dante's *Divina Commedia*, one of which, the City of Dis and the Punishments of Heresy, is shown herein (Pl. 97 A). Preserving to a surprising extent the method of engraving seen in earlier prints by the master, these form an appropriate climax to our whole series of engravings, which commenced with the Coronation of the Virgin, the print supposedly bearing his name. We have it from Vasari that Baldini worked after the designs of Botticelli, and that Botticelli made a series of Dante illustrations which were published; later in this study these Dante illustrations will be identified as a late product of the Baldini-Botticelli collaboration.

PART 5

BALDINI, II

In the preceding Part we isolated a group of copperplate prints and endeavored to show that they had been engraved by one man, whom we believe to be Baccio Baldini. Our inquiry is now directed to determining, so far as it is possible to do so, just where Baldini got his designs.

A casual inspection is enough to show that they come from various sources. Hence, so that we may give order to this phase of our discussion, we separate the Baldini engravings according to the nature of their designs into several groups.

There are, in the first place, those that Baldini himself may have designed early in his career. These show strong German influences. A second group consists of his copies or adaptations of nielli and prints that had been engraved by Finiguerra. Then there is the small group engraved by Baldini after the designs of Botticelli. Engravings based on designs produced in the Finiguerra-Pollaiuolo workshop form still another category. A final group consists of Baldini's copies or adaptations of miscellaneous works of art having contemporary interest.

To begin with the first group — those made after his own compositions — we consider three early engravings that seem likely to have been done by him. These are the Resurrection with a Table to Find Easter, 1461 (detail, Pl. 70 A; Hind, A.I.7); the Gallant and His Mistress Holding a Crown (Pl. 70 B; Hind, A.IV.19); and Virgil the Sorcerer (detail, Pl. 71 C; Hind, A.I.47). In examining these prints, one should remember Vasari's statement that Baldini did not show very much ability as a designer. Certainly these prints are by a draughtsman of that order. Although inept and childish in the drab flow of their compositions, they are yet works of key importance in the annals of Florentine engraving, for all three stem from a similar group of German designs: copperplate prints by the Master of the Banderoles.

The Christ of the Resurrection may be compared with the figure of Adam by the Master of the Banderoles (Pl. 71 A; Lehrs, IV.321.107, 3 A). The reclining female nude at the base of the print of the Gallant and His Mistress, and the figure of Febilla on the pedestal in Virgil the Sorcerer, may be compared with the Nude Woman with a Rose (Pl. 71 B; Lehrs, IV.322.10).

Another print in this first group of Baldini works is the Death and Assumption of the Virgin. When its central panel, the Death of the Virgin (Pl. 73 B), is compared with the Saint Simon (Pl. 73 A; Lehrs, I.224.18), and the Saint Peter (Pl. 73 C; Lehrs, I.221.8), engraved by another anonymous German — known as the Master of the Year 1446 — another similar instance of borrowing is surely evident. Note, for example, how closely the curly head of Saint Peter in the Italian engraving resembles the head of the German Peter, and how Peter's robe in the Italian work is treated in much the same fashion as the Gothic garment worn by Saint Simon.

In the works of Finiguerra and Pollaiuolo we have already seen indications of this German influence, and it is therefore not surprising to find it in more obvious form in supposed works of an inferior designer, Baldini. As we have suggested, it was altogether natural for the Italians to have borrowed as they did, for when they first began print making they could not have known how to go about it. The making of nielli did not give them the experience they needed — although in executing prints the Florentine designers made full use of the niellist's technique — for the tiny scale of the silver plaques demanded a specialized design unsuited for the larger compositions of the copper plates. Hence it is that Baldini, seemingly one of the first Florentines to design prints, found in the work of the German masters the answers to some of the vexing questions facing him.

Among the prints engraved by Baldini at a somewhat later date but still in the German manner, the Vienna Triumphs of Petrarch (Hind, A.I.18–23) would seem to have been designed by Baldini with the exception of one, which was designed by Finiguerra. As we have already seen, the first print of the series, the Triumph of Love (Pl. 82), contains figures similar to those in the Picture-Chronicle drawings (Section III, Part 2). A further comparison of the general composition of the Triumph of Love with that of various drawings in the Chronicle would seem to leave no doubt that Finiguerra was the sole designer of that particular print, except for such minor additions as the cloud forms.

The five remaining Triumphs, on the other hand, are seemingly after Baldini's designs, although, as in the instance of the first series of the Planets, Finiguerra may well have supplied the compositional ideas for all of them. The actual designs are typical of the work of Baldini as we have come to know it. The heads are bedecked in Germanic curls, the hands often look like combs, and there is an almost Gothic torturing of the draperies. Such treatment recalls that found in the design attributed to Baldini for the Death and Assumption of the Virgin (Pl. 72). In one of the Triumphs, that of Fame, three nude prisoners are represented in what is evidently a corrupted version of Pollaiuolo's style. Since Pollaiuolo as well as Finiguerra was an associate of Baldini, this again would be a credible form of borrowing.

The ten prints of the Vienna Passion, another great early series, are stylistically akin to the Triumphs and may also be said to have been designed by Baldini. Like the Triumphs, their designs are based in part on German and Pollaiuolan elements; unlike them, they are seemingly based in part on compositions from the Venetian block-book Passion of about 1450, a work to which nielli engraved by Finiguerra and Baldini already have been related (Section I, Parts 2 and 4).

The various derivative aspects of the Vienna Passion designs are readily apparent. When the Vienna Agony in the Garden (Pl. 75 B; Hind, A.I.25) is compared with the version of the same subject by the Master of the Year 1446 (Pl. 75 A; Lehrs, I.215.1), it is evident that the Italian designer must have been familiar with the German print's composition. This circumstance is repeated in two other instances in the Vienna series: the Entombment and the Pietà (Pls. 76 B and 77 B; Hind, A.I.34 and 33) similarly have their prototypes in engravings by the Master of the Year 1446 (Pls. 76 A and 77 A; Lehrs, I.219.7 and 6). Pollaiuolan inspiration is to be seen in the figures of the Flagellation (detail, Pl. 79; Hind, A.I.28), although the background here is evidently taken from some early German print. Finally the relation between the Vienna Passion and the Venetian block-book Passion is substantiated by several comparisons. To mention one of them, the antecedent for Christ Carrying the Cross (Pl. 78 B; Hind, A.I.30) seems surely to be the earlier, woodcut version (Pl. 78 A). It should be pointed out in this connection that a sulphur cast of the same subject from Finiguerra's Passion series of 1452–1455, now in the Louvre (A. Blum, *Les Nielles*, no. 4), seems equally to have been inspired by the block-book illustration; and it is possible that this niello may have influenced the design of the Vienna Passion print as much as did the block book. In passing one can also note that the treatment of drapery throughout the Vienna Passion seems to be a Baldinian development of this German-inspired Venetian style.

The Mass of Saint Gregory (Pl. 80; Hind, A.I.44), another notable print in the

German style, may also be given to Baldini, for it is related to his designs for the Vienna Passion. As is generally known, it is a variant of a print of the same subject by the Master of the Banderoles (Pl. 81; Lehrs, IV.93.65). Actually the manner in which it varies from its German prototype is just as telling as the way in which it follows it. The figure of the man at the extreme right, for example, while not in the manner of the Master of the Banderoles, also betrays a German origin; its inspiration is to be found in the style of the Master of the Year 1446.

In a number of the Triumph and Passion prints, and in various other prints by Baldini, we find certain mannerisms recurring, two of which particularly deserve mention. Over and over again we come upon the same curiously shaped trees, as in the Entombment from the Passion (Pl. 76 B), their foliage seemingly drawn as with a draughtsman's compass; and the same dartlike cloud forms, as in the Triumph of Love (Pl. 82) and the Pietà from the Passion (Pl. 77 B). Since these occur only in prints attributable to Baldini, they would seem to be hallmarks of his style.

A second group of engravings concerns another phase of Baldini's activity, the republishing of certain notable works engraved by his more distinguished colleague, Maso Finiguerra. Among Baldini's early engravings, the central design of the Coronation of the Virgin (Pl. 68; Hind, A.I.12) is clearly after Maso's pax of the same subject (Pl. 17); and the central design of the Baptism of Christ (Pl. 69; Hind, A.I.10) is based on the composition of a niello Baptism (Pl. 18) engraved by Finiguerra. With these two Baldini prints, therefore, we are faced with an exact parallel to a performance observed in our study of nielli (Section I, Part 4), namely, that the Crucifixion pax in the Bargello (Pl. 33) was Baldini's variant of the niello composition engraved by Finiguerra (Pl. 16).

It is not surprising, then, to find that the second series of the Planets was the result of the very same procedure; indeed these prints are no more than Baldini's variants of the set already described as having been engraved by Finiguerra (Section IV, Part 3). As shown in the Three Humanists (Pl. 83), a detail of the Planet Jupiter (Hind, A.III.2,b), the style of these second Planets naturally differs considerably from the more characteristically Baldinian manner of the Triumph and Passion prints; nevertheless there is a certain thread binding them together: I refer especially to Baldini's consistent treatment of minor architectural decoration.

In a similar fashion the second Procession to Calvary and the Crucifixion (Hind, A.II.7) is a copy — and not in this instance a variant — of Finiguerra's print of the same subject (Hind, A.II.8). Good copy that it is, when we compare the ornament of the shield held by the warrior in the foreground of each print, we discover that one is typically Finiguerran, and the other just as typically Baldinian.

At this point we come to another group of Baldini engravings; we also come upon a new personality. Little enough is known of the young Sandro Botticelli. He was, Vasari tells us, apprenticed by his father to a goldsmith named Botticello.

Seemingly the youngster proved to be an able apprentice who devoted his time wholly to design, showing such promise that he was eventually placed with Fra Filippo Lippi to learn the painter's craft. During these years, according to our reading of the evidence, Botticelli began to create designs that were used by copperplate engravers.

There are various indications in his early paintings that Botticelli had been with Pollaiuolo. Sandro's first documented painting is the Fortezza, which he executed in 1470 for the Mercatanzia of Florence. It is one of a series of the seven Virtues, the other six of which were painted by Antonio's brother, Piero. In its style the Fortezza fits in agreeably with the other paintings by the Pollaiuolo brothers. Discussing this relationship, Bernard Berenson in his *Drawings of the Florentine Painters* (Vol. I, p. 21, n. 2) observes: "It could have been no mere accident that led to Botticelli's painting one panel in a series to be done by the Pollaiuolo. Does it not point to his close connection with them, or even to his having been at the time in their employ?" Mr. Berenson continues that "it is not likely that Botticelli would have been given his commission, unless it had been felt that his panel would not be out of harmony with the others. So we are forced to one of two conclusions: either Sandro was just then still on terms of close connection with the Pollaiuolo, or he had been, and the similarity of his style to theirs was so notorious that he was expected to paint in their character." From the evidence of certain engravings, I think it will become clear that, as Mr. Berenson suggests, Botticelli had been in close association with Pollaiuolo, and that it was an association that may have commenced as early as 1465, when Botticelli was twenty years old.

If, as I believe, the Judgment Hall of Pilate (Pl. 106) was designed by Botticelli, it was surely made while he was still strongly under the influence of Pollaiuolo. In this print there seem to be many signs pointing directly to Pollaiuolo. There is, for example, at the left side of this engraving a Flagellation delineated in a graceful, dreamy manner that seems prophetic of Botticelli's mature style, yet in everything but mood it is similar to the sterner Pollaiuolan version of the subject found in niello work on the Metropolitan's cross (Pl. 25 a). Also, when we compare the figures in the detail showing Pilate washing his hands (Pl. 85) with the central Pollaiuolan figure in Finiguerra's engraving of the Planet Mercury (Hind, A.III.6 a) a general correspondence of style is again apparent.

If the Judgment Hall of Pilate is after a design by Botticelli, so also is the Conversion of Paul (detail, Pl. 105 a; Hind, A.II.10), another print showing markedly Pollaiuolan traits, softened, as in the Pilate composition, by Botticelli's inherent elegance of expression. Here, too, is a feeling for the reality of landscape that is unlike anything found in contemporary engravings, and that, as we shall see, presages Botticelli's landscapes in his designs for prints engraved by Rosselli. And just as Pilate's temple is a reasonable structure, the walled city in the distance of the

Conversion of Paul is substantial and orderly; it is far from the hit-or-miss affairs of similar representations in the Planets and Finiguerra's Chronicle.

There is good reason then to consider the Judgment Hall of Pilate and the Conversion of Paul as having been designed by Botticelli. On the basis of Baldini's engraving technique, they seem later than the second series of the Planets, that is, after 1464–1465. On the basis of their compositions, however, they can be no later than the early engravings made jointly by Rosselli and Botticelli. Since, as we shall see in the next Part of this study, the Rosselli engravings may be dated before 1475, a date of 1465–1475 may reasonably be assigned to Baldini's Pilate and Paul engravings.

There are still other instances of Botticelli's collaboration with Baldini. One of these is a plate of eight border panels with arabesque designs (Hind, A.III.9, a), which are clearly later additions to Finiguerra's series of the Planets. As we saw in Part 4 this series had in part been reworked by Baldini. The border panels differ from the only printed arabesques thought to be of the early 1460s — the candelabra flanking the Finiguerra-Pollaiuolo engraving of the Beheading of a Captive (Pl. 65) — in that they are less crude, and more correctly classical. On the other hand, they are similar in composition to the border panels (Hind, B.I.17) for the series of the Life of the Virgin and of Christ, which as we shall see was engraved by Rosselli after Botticelli's designs between about 1465 and 1475. Although they can be dated no earlier than the Rosselli series, they need not be dated any later.

Another instance of Botticelli's collaboration with Baldini concerns the nineteen plates for Dante's *Divina Commedia* of 1481 with a commentary by Cristoforo Landino (Hind, A.V.2 [1–19]). We have it on the authority of Vasari that Botticelli made a series of designs for the *Divine Comedy* which were put into print; and we have the book. These Dante illustrations correspond closely with drawings for the same subject which Sandro made, possibly more than a decade later, for Lorenzo di Pierfrancesco Medici. When one of the engravings, such as the City of Dis and the Punishments of Heresy (Pl. 97 A; Hind, A.V.2 [10,1]), is compared with the Botticelli drawing from the Medici series in the Vatican Library (Pl. 97 B), there can be no doubt about the attribution. Nevertheless, in comparison with the broad-manner engravings which (as we shall see in Section IV, Part 6) had by that time already been produced by Rosselli and Botticelli, they are coarsely done. Strident Baldinian details of line and decoration continually obtrude. It is evident therefore that Baldini vulgarized Botticelli's designs, giving to them some of the by then archaic character of the Finiguerra-Pollaiuolo workshop from which he stemmed. In view of all this, it is not difficult to understand why the *Divine Comedy* illustrations have remained such a puzzle in the annals of engraving.

As we come to the next design group in this analysis of Baldini prints, we reach the point where it is well to define the expression "Finiguerra-Pollaiuolo workshop." There is no documentary evidence that such a bottega ever existed. But whatever its name, and whether it functioned under the sponsorship of Bartolommeo di Piero di Salì, with whom both Finiguerra and Pollaiuolo are known to have worked, it would seem an undoubted fact that there was such a shop, and that Pollaiuolo, Finiguerra, Baldini, and Botticelli were all at one time or another active in it. It probably was not a tightly knit organization. Pollaiuolo, for example, seems to have lost interest in prints after a few years of activity in the field; Finiguerra's career was cut short by his early death in 1464; Botticelli was a late arrival and an infrequent, if important, contributor; Baldini, who more and more looms up as a central figure in this study, alone continued to produce engravings over a long span of years until his death sometime in the 1480s. From time to time the workshop included others, masters or assistants whose names are unknown to us but whose works bear a similar stamp. For want of a better term, therefore, we may describe their productions as of the Finiguerra-Pollaiuolo workshop.

Among these workshop designs engraved by Baldini are such single prints as the Saint Catherine of Siena (Pl. 87 A; Hind, A.I.66), and the Filippesque Virgin and Child Standing before a Throne with Saint Sebastian and Saint Catherine (Pl. 86 A; Hind, A.II.25). There are also the two series of the twenty-four Prophets (Hind, C.I.1,a–24,a) and the twelve Sibyls (Hind, C.II.1,a–12,a); and these, needless to add, are the early, fine-manner Prophets and Sibyls.

As we have remarked before in our study of engraving technique, Baldini's Virgin and Child Standing before a Throne (Pl. 86 A) is nearly identical in the treatment of architectural decoration with the Judgment Hall of Pilate (detail, Pl. 85) and with the Sibyl Agrippa (Pl. 86 B). And this, we may now observe, is a matter of style as well as technique inasmuch as it may represent Baldini's contribution to the design of these prints. In addition, the Saint Catherine of Siena (Pl. 87 A) bears close affinities to the Pilate print and to another of the Sibyls, the Erythrean (Pl. 87 B).

According to the evidence, then, the Sibyls may be said to have been engraved by Baldini at about the time of the making of the Judgment Hall of Pilate, that is, about 1465–1475. The same may also be said for the Prophets, which form a companion series to the Sibyls and are identical to them in style of design.

A number of Prophets and Sibyls show the influence of Pollaiuolo and Botticelli; some of them also seem to be in the style of the Chronicle drawings, although their designs could not be the works of Finiguerra, who had died before they were executed. The composition of one of the Prophets, the Noah (Pl. 89; Hind, C.I.1), like that of so many of Finiguerra's drawings, seems to have been based on Ghiberti's relief of God the Father made in 1450 for the hospital of Santa Maria Nuova in Florence (Pl. 88). And a number of the others are known to be after German engravings by the Master E. S. and Martin Schongauer, whose works had by then come to Florence. Among the Prophets and Sibyls, obviously, there is no consistency of style;

nor in the light of our knowledge is there any eclectic master who, like Finiguerra in the instance of the Picture-Chronicle, can be credited with their designs. Possibly more than one master worked on them; at any event they can securely be attributed to the Finiguerra-Pollaiuolo workshop.

Among the other Baldini prints based on designs from the Finiguerra-Pollaiuolo workshop is the group known to be related to drawings in the Picture-Chronicle, which had been left incomplete in midsummer of 1464. They are surely adapted from the Chronicle, and may have been made at any time between 1465 and, say, 1480. In this category are several of the circular prints in the so-called Otto series, two characteristic examples of which are Judith with the Head of Holophernes (Pl. 91; Hind, A.IV.1), a print reminiscent of the Chronicle drawing of Theseus and the Amazon (detail, Pl. 90; S. Colvin, *Florentine Picture-Chronicle*, pl. 39); and Jason and Medea (Pl. 93; Hind, A.IV.6), the model for which is the Chronicle drawing of the same subject (Pl. 92; Colvin, *op. cit.*, pl. 58). It may be noted that a number of these prints, such as the Woman with a Unicorn (Hind, A.IV.4), are in style closely related to the three illustrations from the *Monte Sancto di Dio*, especially to that of the Holy Mountain (Hind, A.V.1 [1]). Since this volume was published in 1477, it becomes a useful guide for the dating of various engravings designed in the Finiguerra-Pollaiuolo workshop.

A number of other prints, quite apart from the Otto series, were inspired by the Picture-Chronicle. The engraving of the Cretan Labyrinth (Hind, A.II.16) is plainly a variant of a Chronicle illustration (Colvin, *op. cit.*, pls. 46 and 47), and so also is Baldini's Story of the Creation (Pl. 95; Hind, A.II.1). In the tradition of Maso, the designer of the latter print has seemingly adapted his chief character, God the Father, from the figure of Moses on Ghiberti's ''Gates of Paradise'' (Pl. 94). He appears to have taken the representation of the Creation of Eve from the same doorway or from a nielloed version of it (Pl. 2 B). Other details, such as the mermaid in the stream, and the weedy treatment of the foreground, are lifted from the Picture-Chronicle. A more synthetic composition can scarcely be envisaged. Nor could any print be more thoroughly the product of a designer of the Finiguerra-Pollaiuolo workshop.

To round out the Baldini story, we now consider the group of prints that reveals our master as a publisher who would seemingly reproduce any subject demanded. Just as he had made prints after engravings by Finiguerra, he issued copies or variants of a number of paintings or other compositions of contemporary interest. The sources of some of these prints are known; the sources of others remain a mystery.

We find, for example, that the Inferno According to Dante (Hind, A.I.60) is after the fourteenth-century fresco attributed to Orcagna in the Campo Santo at Pisa. In style it is near to the Vienna Triumphs and Passion series, and also to the Mass of Saint Gregory, and like them may be dated about 1463–1464. It is a print of unusual interest in that Baldini produced variants of it on two later occasions, once in a simplified version of the subject (Hind, A.I.59), and again, in still simpler form, as one of his three illustrations for the *Monte Sancto di Dio* of 1477 (Pl. 96; Hind, A.V.1 [3]). Since more than a decade elapsed between the first and final variants, the differences between them would seem to be of consequence in showing the development of his style. In the earliest example, seemingly made about 1463–1464, Baldini drew the various figures in the composition as if he were imitating the Master of the Year 1446. In the 1477 version all Germanic elements have vanished. And although the crabbed Baldinian line remains in the final version, he has so reduced the complexities of the Campo Santo fresco that his engraving does not seem inappropriate as an example of renaissance book illustration.

Another early reproductive print by Baldini is Dante as the Poet of the Divine Comedy (Hind, A.I.61), his version of a fresco executed in 1465 by Domenico di Michelino for the Florentine Duomo. Judging from the Germanic elements still to be observed in the Baldini manner, the plate may have been engraved shortly after the painting was finished.

Several other closely related prints may be cited as late examples in this group of Baldini copies and variants. They may indeed be dated between 1481, the year of the making of the Dante illustrations, and 1487, which may have been the time of Baldini's death. These prints include Tobias and the Angel (Pl. 98 B; Hind, A.I.82); Christ on the Cross between the Virgin and Saint John (Pl. 98 A; Hind, A.I.83); and the Story of the Dead King and His Sons (Pl. 99; Hind, A.I.52). The first appears to be after a panel in the Uffizi believed to have been painted by Botticini about 1475. The origins of the designs for the other two are unknown. Stylistically, however, the Christ on the Cross relates to a woodcut from a *Missale Romanum* published by Octavianus Scotus in Venice, August 31, 1482, and certainly would seem to be of no earlier date (Prince d'Essling, *Les Missels imprimés à Venise de 1481 à 1600*, Paris, 1896, pp. 58 ff.). The Story of the Dead King and His Sons, which from the standpoint of engraving technique is near the Dante illustrations of 1481, would seem in view of the treatment of its architectural background to be based on some such composition as Perugino's fresco of the Delivery of the Keys to Saint Peter in the Sistine Chapel in Rome, a work executed in 1482. Thus a date of about 1481–1487 (?) seems to be in order for all three.

These add a last note to the Baldini story, showing the final phase of certain mannerisms which we have earlier referred to as hallmarks of Baldini's style. The dartlike cloud forms of the Baldini prints made some twenty years previously have now become the multiple darts that dominate the sky. And the foliage that was once drawn in perfect circles as with a compass is now done more subtly, and tactile values have replaced the former flat mode of representation.

PART 6

ROSSELLI AND BOTTICELLI

The Rosselli-Botticelli collaboration, the last of the print-making partnerships to be considered in this essay, may be approached by studying the evidence that would seem to relate a large group of broad-manner engravings to their designer, whom we believe to be Botticelli, and then by examining the evidence relating this same group to their engraver, whom we believe to be Rosselli.

We begin with Sandro Botticelli, whose engravings made in collaboration with Baldini have already been dealt with in the preceding Part. The works we are now to consider seem to reveal him as under the influence of Fra Filippo Lippi, the master who has played a determining rôle behind the scenes throughout this study. Such a development in Sandro's style is hardly surprising, for we know that he worked with Filippo during the late 1460s on the great fresco series in the Duomo at Prato. According to Vasari, Botticelli's apprenticeship with Filippo marked a turning point in the young artist's career. For in the Lippi shop, "devoting himself heart and soul to the art [of painting], Sandro followed and imitated his master so well that . . . he soon rose to such rank as none would have expected of him."

Among the designs for engravings relatable to Botticelli during or soon after his association with Lippi are four notable series. Two of them are the twenty-four Prophets (Hind, C.I.1,b–24,b) and the twelve Sibyls (Hind, C.II.1,b–12,b). To the extent that they are revisions of the two fine-manner series of the same subjects that Baldini had earlier engraved after models from the Finiguerra-Pollaiuolo workshop, their designs seem to relate to Botticelli. The two other series presumably after the latter's designs are the seventeen prints from the Life of the Virgin and of Christ (Hind, B.I.1–17) and the six Triumphs of Petrarch (Hind, B.II.1–6). Also in this group are the following single prints: the two versions of the Deluge (Hind, B.III.1 and 3); the Adoration of the Magi (Hind, B.III.2); Moses on Mount Sinai and the Brazen Serpent (Hind, B.III.5); Solomon and the Queen of Sheba (Hind, B.III.4); and David and Goliath (Hind, B.III.6).

Before endeavoring to show that Botticelli was concerned with these prints, we present evidence to indicate that all of them do in fact belong together. When, for example, we compare the Nativity (Pl. 101; Hind, B.I.3), from the Life of the Virgin and of Christ, with a detail from the single print of the Adoration of the Magi (detail, Pl. 100; Hind, B.III.2), we discover that the figures of the Virgin are similar, that there are the same stables with the same drowsy animals, and that even the

68

small figures on the hillsides are treated in a similar fashion. And when we compare a detail from the print of Christ Bearing the Cross (Pl. 102 A; Hind, B.I.9), also from the series of the Life of the Virgin and of Christ, with one from the single print of David and Goliath (Pl. 102 B; Hind, B.III.6), we find that the crowds of soldiers are similarly represented, even the harnesses on their horses being depicted in the same way.

Another such comparison involves examples from the series of the Life of the Virgin and of Christ and that of the Prophets. The first is a detail from the engraving of Christ Disputing with the Doctors (Pl. 103 B; Hind, B.I.5); the second is the prophet Obadiah (Pl. 103 A; Hind, C.I.16,b). In the two engravings the same treatment of the seated figure is to be observed, the same features, and the same expressions.

Or again, let us compare still another detail from the series of the Life of the Virgin and of Christ with a detail from one of the Triumphs of Petrarch. The former is a section of landscape in the Assumption (Pl. 104 A; Hind, B.I.14); the latter is a similar section from the Triumph of Love (Pl. 104 B; Hind, B.II.1). In both instances the landscape backgrounds with their hills, houses, and trees are designed in much the same way.

For a final comparison, we call attention to the Visitation and the Presentation in the Temple (Hind, B.I.2 and 4), two prints from the Life of the Virgin and of Christ, and the single print of Solomon and the Queen of Sheba (Hind, B.III.4). These show the same knowing and delicately balanced treatment of the architectural setting, which, it may be noted, characterizes all prints in this group in which architectural elements are present.

Granted then that these several prints show a single source of design, what proof is there that the designer was Botticelli? There are two ways of approaching the problem: one by following the line of evidence concerning Botticelli's relationship to Pollaiuolo; and the other by following the line of evidence concerning his relationship to Fra Filippo Lippi.

We have already seen that Botticelli supplied the designs for Baldini's fine-manner engravings of the Judgment Hall of Pilate and the Conversion of Paul. We therefore seek a relationship between these and the broad-manner prints now under consideration, and, unless I am far wrong, there is no difficulty in finding it. For surely the composition of the Pollaiuolo-inspired Judgment Hall of Pilate (Pl. 106) bears a more than passing resemblance to that of Solomon and the Queen of Sheba (Pl. 107). Is there not in both the same static grouping of graceful figures, and the same symmetrically planned architectural setting? Similarly, the Pollaiuolan Conversion of Paul may be related to the David and Goliath. In these two prints there is not only a like feeling for landscape, but even a resemblance between the designs of the walled cities represented on the horizons (Pl. 105 A and B). Clearly, then, a close relationship links the two Baldini-Botticelli engravings to those in the broad-manner group.

In our second approach to the problem — the tracing of a connection between Botticelli and Filippo Lippi — we again have a good deal to go on. It must, for instance, be accounted a significant fact that the design of the first print in the series of the Life of the Virgin and of Christ, the Annunciation (Pl. 109 A; Hind, B.I.1), is a free adaptation of Lippi's painting of the same subject (Pl. 108) in the Florentine church of San Lorenzo. One can hardly say of it, "How unlike Sandro to appropriate another's design," since years later, in 1488, he again made use of the very same one. On that occasion he adapted the Lippi model for his painted panel of the Annunciation which now hangs in the Uffizi (Pl. 109 B).

Consider another example: the figure of the dancing Salome (Pl. 110 A) in the great fresco of the Banquet of Herod, a work painted by Lippi in 1464 or shortly thereafter for the Duomo at Prato; this would seem to be the direct inspiration for one of the dancing maidens in the Triumph of Love (Pl. 110 B; Hind, B.II.1). Despite the intrusion of the engraver's personality — concerning which we will have more to say presently — we find in both a similar pose and a like treatment of clothing.

Two other telling instances may be cited. One centers upon the Presentation in the Temple (detail, Pl. 111 B; Hind, B.I.4), which is certainly very like the painting of the same subject in the Museum at Prato (Pl. 111 A), one of a series of predella panels made by Filippo's follower Fra Diamante (M. Pittaluga, *Filippo Lippi*, pl. 176). Scholars have observed that the Fra Diamante panel is based on a painting of the Circumcision in the church of Santo Spirito in Prato, executed by Lippi about 1467–1468 with the probable aid of Fra Diamante. The predella panel painting is therefore of a later date; according to Dr. Pittaluga it should be placed about 1468–1470. It seems possible to us that both Fra Diamante's predella panel and the Presentation find their source in the painting of the Circumcision, and that both may be dated as early as 1468–1470. It hardly seems likely that the engraving could have been made after 1475.

In a similar fashion the single print of the Adoration of the Magi (Hind, B.III.2) is related to a second panel from the predella series in the Museum at Prato (Pittaluga, *op. cit.*, pl. 175). As in the case of the Presentation in the Temple, a third work enters the story: the Adoration of the Magi in the National Gallery in London, one of the first paintings known to be by Botticelli, although it is not securely dated (Adolfo Venturi, *Botticelli*, Paris, 1926, pl. I). Despite this uncertainty as to date, the Fra Diamante version surely derives from it, and may, like the Presentation in the Prato Museum, be placed about 1468–1470. Hence, we may assume that Botticelli's painting had been painted earlier, perhaps, like the Santo Spirito Presentation, about 1467–1468. Significantly enough, the engraving is more closely related to

Botticelli's painting than to that by Fra Diamante. Aside from its connection with a known painting by Botticelli, its close kinship with Fra Diamante underlines the bond between the broad-manner engravings and the work being carried on at Prato under the aegis of Fra Filippo.

On the basis of these several comparisons, we may conclude that the broad-manner engravings listed above were all designed while the young Botticelli was strongly under the influence of Lippi. Fra Filippo died in 1469, and the engravings surely cannot have been made much later since they do not compare in style with the paintings Botticelli is known to have made after 1470. It seems safe to say that the inclusive dates of about 1465–1475 would apply to all of them.

Although Botticelli's great period as a print designer was seemingly before 1475, it may be noted, in order to complete our report, that a few other broad-manner engravings directly or indirectly based on his designs were made after 1475. Such are the Last Judgment (Hind, B.III.7), the Preaching of Fra Marco (Hind, B.III.8), the Last Supper (Hind, B.III.11), the Virgin and Child Enthroned between Saint Helena and Saint Michael (Hind, B.III.9), and the Assumption of the Virgin (Hind, B.III.10). A few remarks about some of these should suffice to show their connection with Botticelli.

The print of the Preaching of Fra Marco of Santa Maria in Gallo was evidently the one described by Vasari as being by Botticelli. The biographer called it, however, the Triumph of Faith as Effected by Fra Girolamo Savonarola, perhaps being misled by the facts that a Monte di Pietà is represented in the composition and that Savonarola had founded a Monte di Pietà as a bank for the Florentine poor. No such Savonarola print as Vasari described is known, nor is such a subject found in the Rosselli inventory, a list which, as we shall presently see, contains entries apparently corresponding to every engraving related to Botticelli, including the one of the Preaching of Fra Marco. It may be added that, although this print can be described as being after the design of Botticelli, one detail in it, the view of the Mediterranean basin in the distance, calls to mind the various maps known to have been made by Rosselli. In the light of our study of Finiguerra and Baldini, such an addition by Rosselli to the design would not be unexpected if the Fra Marco print were engraved by him.

To mention one other of these later engravings, the Virgin and Child Enthroned between Saint Helena and Saint Michael is related to various paintings with the Madonna theme by Botticelli, in particular to the altarpiece in the Uffizi of the Virgin and Child Enthroned between Angels and Saints (Venturi, op. cit., pl. LXXX), a work executed in 1483, and the Virgin and Child Enthroned between Saint John the Baptist and Saint John the Evangelist, formerly in the Kaiser Friedrich Museum in Berlin (Venturi, op. cit., pl. XCI). The relationship of this print to Botticelli's work may have been indirect; its actual designer could even have been an anonymous master working eclectically in the manner of Botticelli.

71

Now we come to the problem of the engraver, Botticelli's partner in this enterprise, whom we believe to be Francesco Rosselli. Little is known about him. He was a contemporary of Botticelli's, and of about the same age, having been born in 1445 or 1447. He was still living in 1508. In his day Francesco Rosselli had a reputation as an illuminator and printer (*miniatore e stampatore*); he was also known as a cartographer (*cosmographus*). One map, the Map of the World (Hind, G.6), is actually signed by him. A number of others that figure in the inventory made after the death in 1525 of Alessandro Rosselli, his son and successor, may also be presumed to have been Francesco's work. There is, however, no precise documentary evidence to show that he ever engraved copperplate prints.

Nevertheless the question of the relation of Rosselli to broad-manner engraving has long intrigued students of the subject. On page 11 of the first volume of *Early Italian Engraving*, Arthur M. Hind observed: "The wind faces in Rosselli's *Map of the World* are related in style to the Broad-Manner group, and the presence of so large a proportion of Broad-Manner engravings in the [Rosselli] inventory, tempts me to think that he may have been the engraver of various plates of this group . . . Some support is given to the attribution to Rosselli of the engraving of certain Broad-Manner prints by the comparison of detail, e.g., the large and small lettering of the place names, and the title and signature in the cartouche of the *Map of the World* (Hind, G.6) with the lettering on the *Preaching of Fra Marco* (Hind, B.III.8). Moreover the map of the Mediterranean Basin in the background of this engraving is in Rosselli's style, and may have been borrowed from him, if not engraved by him. And the view of Rome in the background of the large *Assumption* (Hind, B.III.10) very probably derives from the lost *View of Rome* noted in the Inventory, which was almost certainly Rosselli's work."

To the relationships observed by Mr. Hind, another may be added, one that is perhaps of even more significance for the purposes of this study. It has to do with a broad-manner engraving, the only extant part of a large view of Florence (Hind, B.III.18). There can, I think, be no disputing Mr. Hind's analysis of this print when he writes (*op. cit.*, Vol. I, p. 146): "In view of the facts that Francesco Rosselli was a notable cartographer, that the inventory of his son's stock contained this engraving, and that an engraved *Map of the World* signed by Rosselli is preserved (Hind, G.6), there is every reason to regard the present engraved view as by his hand."

What interests us is that Rosselli's engraved view of Florence is related to certain prints among the Botticellian broad-manner engravings. We have already observed that the Assumption of the Virgin (detail, Pl. 104 A) and the Triumph of Love (detail, Pl. 104 B) are related in respect to their landscape backgrounds. And now we discover that the very same manner of treating the landscape occurs in the view of Florence (detail, Pl. 112 A). We must conclude then that all three prints were engraved by Rosselli, and, since the view of Florence is of a later date than the engravings with which it is compared — it was made after 1480 — that Rosselli borrowed from his experience with Botticelli to create such a composition. We must also conclude that just as Rosselli was the engraver of these three prints, so he was the engraver of all the broad-manner engravings made after Botticelli's designs. Technically these broad-manner prints may not be differentiated; the same mannerisms, which may be attributed to the engraver, appear in all of them.

Hence it follows that if Botticelli made all the designs and Rosselli engraved all the plates, we must accept the existence of the Botticelli-Rosselli collaboration.

This conclusion is, I think, immeasurably strengthened by the evidence contained within the famous Rosselli inventory, drawn up following the death in 1525 of Francesco's son, Alessandro. The inventory consists of 26 items relating to printed impressions from wood blocks and metal plates; 34 items relating to printer's equipment, books, et cetera; 30 items relating to wood blocks; and 49 items relating to metal plates, of which all except three — these are of tin and brass and do not figure in our story — are copper. It is these 46 copper plates that now concern us.

Of these 46 entries, 20 refer to maps and navigation charts which were surely the work of the cosmographer Francesco Rosselli. Of the remaining 26 entries, 14 (including 4 Crucifixions and 2 or 3 ornament prints) are not identifiable. Significantly, the remaining 12 are all related to prints that on the basis of their design have in the course of this study been attributed to Sandro Botticelli. And what is equally significant, with one exception, *all* the prints that have been related to Botticelli in this study, both in the fine manner and in the broad manner, have their respective entries in this inventory. The exception is the series of illustrations from the *Divine Comedy* of 1481, but the plates for these were executed for a book publisher (Nicolaus Laurentii, Alamanus), not for a publisher of prints, and naturally would not be found in such a listing.

Because of their importance for our study, we give these entries in detail. In reading them, it will be remembered that, as was usually the case, the metal plates were engraved on both front and back surfaces. The twelve entries are as follows:

Item 34: *1° cienacholo, da l'altra banda 1ª nostra donna.* The Last Supper may be identified as Hind, B.III.11, and the Madonna engraving may be Hind, B.III.9.

Item 37: *1° diluvio di foglio reale chol tenpio di salamone.* The Deluge is Hind, B.III.3; and the Solomon and the Queen of Sheba is Hind, B.III.4.

Item 38: *1ª morte d'ugolia, da altra banda da storia di muisè, inn un foglio reale.* The David and Goliath is Hind, B.III.6; and the Moses on Mount Sinai is Hind, B.III.5.

Item 39: *1° diluvio d'un foglio reale, e una natività.* The Deluge is Hind, B.III.1; and the Nativity (Adoration of the Magi) is Hind, B.III.2.

Item 40: *1° giudizo d'un foglio reale, e'l monte di piatà.* The Last Judgment is Hind, B.III.7; and the Fra Marco and the Works of Mercy (with a representation of a mountain of money, inscribed Mons Pietatis) is Hind, B.III.8.

Item 42: *1° tenpio di pilato, chon meza inchoronazione di nostra donna di 2 fogli reali.* The Judgment Hall of Pilate is Hind, A.II.9; and the engraving of the Coronation of the Virgin is presumably lost. Mr. Hind supposes that this was an engraving made after Botticelli's painting of the same subject which is now in the Uffizi.

Item 43: *1ᵃ asensione di 6* (corrected from 4) *fogli reali inn un pezo.* This is probably the Assumption of the Virgin; Hind, B.III.10.

Item 54: *1ᵃ chonsizione di san pagolo, in foglio reale.* This is the Conversion of Paul; Hind, A.II.10.

Item 71: *17 pezi di sobile e profeti, dopie.* These are the broad-manner Prophets and Sibyls; Hind, C.I.1,b–24,b and C.II.1,b–12,b.

Item 72: *1° giuocho del trionfo del petrarcha in 3 pezi.* These are the six broad-manner Triumphs of Petrarch; Hind, B.II.1–6.

Item 73: *1° giuocho di pianeti chon loro fregi, in 4 pezi.* These are the fine-manner Planets (Hind, A.III.1,a–7,a) engraved by Finiguerra, to which were added the border panels designed by Botticelli and engraved by Baldini (Hind, A.III.9,a).

Item 75: *10 forme di rosai dopi, stanpe di 1/2 foglio chomune.* These are the fifteen scenes (from the Rosary) of the Life of the Virgin and of Christ; Hind, B.I.1–15. Two series of border panels evidently went with the set; Hind, B.I.16 and 17. Three other prints seem to have existed which are unaccounted for.

There are, it may be noted, a few additional subjects in the Rosselli list that may or may not relate to existing prints. Item 51, for example, a Saint George, may be the print listed by Mr. Hind as B.III.13. It was surely engraved by Rosselli, reason enough for its inclusion; and its design may possibly have stemmed from a Botticellian model. The case for other items would seem to be less favorable. It would not seem that item 74, the Saint Mary Magdalen, can be related to a known print. The one early engraving of the Magdalen (Hind, A.II.24) not only is not designed by Botticelli, but is not engraved by Rosselli. For the same reasons item 79, a Tobias, cannot be identified with either of the two fine-manner engravings of Tobias and the Angel (Hind, A.I.82 and 83).

All in all, it would seem from our study of the Rosselli inventory that Alessandro possessed a complete set of the Botticelli plates, in both the fine and broad manners, just as he had the plates of all of his father's maps and charts. It appears, too, that Francesco not only engraved most of the prints that Botticelli designed, but also published all the Botticelli prints. Here surely is evidence of their collaboration.

In conclusion, we may briefly inquire into the nature of Rosselli's rôle as interpreter of Botticelli through the agency of his engraved line. Unfortunately, no early drawing by Botticelli exists that was reproduced by Rosselli, and therefore we have no precise basis for comparison. Nor do we have comparable variants of one design engraved by Rosselli and another master, which, if they existed, might well have given us more insight into Rosselli's methods.

74

Nevertheless, both Finiguerra and Baldini set a pattern presumably followed by Rosselli, from which certain conclusions can be drawn. We have seen how Finiguerra gave Pollaiuolo's designs a new quality on the copper plate, and how Baldini altered designs with seemingly little compunction. And as was the case with Finiguerra, all of Rosselli's engravings possess a definite character, at once consistent and assured. Yet the very degree to which that character is definite represents a distortion of the original design. Such a distortion would seemingly account for the loss of grace and fluidity, and for a certain childishness of form, elements that characterize the prints of Rosselli and that could hardly have been present in Botticelli's own drawings. It may indeed have been this that caused Vasari to note that Botticelli's designs had all been engraved badly, in a *"cattiva maniera."*

Be that as it may, such was the inevitable penalty of the collaborative system of print making. Vasari seems to have put his finger on it when he remarked in the passage quoted in our Preface, that try as he would, the engraver could never quite capture the essence of the design he was recording on his copper plate.

CONCLUSION

CONCLUSION

In this essay we have followed the interweaving careers of five masters: Finiguerra, Pollaiuolo, Baldini, Botticelli, and Rosselli. From them we have developed a theory for the early histories of niello work and copperplate engraving in renaissance Florence. Since this theory has a significance of its own above and beyond the histories of these five masters, I venture in these final pages briefly to summarize it.

We began with a study of the works of Maso Finiguerra, and found that by the early 1450s this master was producing nielli more remarkable for the technical proficiency displayed in their manufacture than for the virtue of their design. Maso was one of those artists who find their strength in the works of others, and a number of his nielli are shadowy reflections of the bronze reliefs by his master Lorenzo Ghiberti. But Ghiberti died in 1455 and Maso was soon forced to look elsewhere for support. Before the year 1460 he found it in the person of his somewhat younger colleague, Antonio Pollaiuolo, with whom he was associated in the bottega of the goldsmith Bartolommeo di Piero di Salì. When Maso became a master in his own right, he was far more than a sponger on the work of others. In a sense he had become an impresario. He seems to have skillfully channeled Pollaiuolo's talents as a draughtsman so that together they created works that neither of them would have done individually. For a period of about five years, ending with Maso's death in the summer of 1464, Finiguerra and Pollaiuolo collaborated in producing numerous nielli, the former presumably suggesting, and finally engraving, the designs delineated at least in part by the latter. These two were so busy and successful — and their surviving works show that their success was fully merited — that on one occasion at least they had to call upon the aid of Baccio Baldini, a follower of Maso.

Our study also showed that as *maestri di disegno* Finiguerra and Pollaiuolo worked together in 1463 or 1464 on a commission related not to goldsmithery, but to intarsia work. Maso is known to have designed certain intarsia panels for the Sacristy in the Florentine Duomo. He was aided in this work by his partner, for even during his last years Maso was still a designer of uncertain talent, and still in need of help from a more knowing hand.

His weakness as a draughtsman, which prevents him from now being considered as one of the true masters of the quattrocento, and the rather childish charm of his discursive linear medium which may have made him a popular artist in his own day, were both revealed to us in his Florentine Picture-Chronicle. Done in the final years of his life, this work is almost autobiographical in character. In itself it is lively and amusing, obviously created by a genial if uninspired talent. Yet it is a work of real importance, for in its curious way it stands as a landmark in the history of Florentine art. The evidence to be read upon its pages casts new light upon the origins of copperplate engraving in Florence. Through the Chronicle, for example, we have determined the true position of Pollaiuolo's Battle of the Naked Men as being among the earliest of all Florentine engravings. The same source also gave us a clue that eventually led us to the authors of the Vienna Triumphs of Petrarch, for the first print in that celebrated series was identified as having been designed by Finiguerra at the time when he was working on the Chronicle.

When we turned our attention exclusively to engravings, we noted that, in addition to designing and engraving the Battle of the Naked Men, Pollaiuolo produced at the behest of Finiguerra various drawings which the latter engraved on copper. Chief among these were the first series of the Planets, and the double print of the Triumph of Bacchus and Ariadne. Unfortunately, the Finiguerra-Pollaiuolo partnership, which might have been so wonderfully fruitful, was suddenly ended in midsummer of 1464 by Maso's death. No evidence was found to show that Antonio continued his interest in engraving after the loss of his associate.

But Pollaiuolo and Finiguerra had not been alone in the field. Baccio Baldini, who was surely in their entourage, had as early as 1460 or 1461 begun to make engravings, both as designer and engraver. He was, however, an inferior draughtsman, although he seems to have tried to become a good one. His best designs were five of the six panels of the Vienna Triumphs of Petrarch (the other being the work of Finiguerra) and the ten prints of the Vienna Passion. These we found to be most revealing, for they showed Baldini's deep-rooted dependence upon the designs of early German masters, a dependence shared even by Finiguerra and Pollaiuolo. Such a link between German and Italian engraving, even though confined to a few brief years, serves to underline the quandary of the Florentine masters when in about 1460 they first began to create designs for the new and unfamiliar art of engraving.

If Baldini was lacking in inventive ability as a designer, he was not wanting in persistence as an engraver. Indeed his real career was engraving, and in the later 1460s and throughout the 1470s he seems to have restricted himself to that activity. By 1465 he had engraved the Vienna Triumphs of Petrarch, the Vienna Passion, and the second series of Finiguerra's Planets. Shortly thereafter he engraved the fine-manner Prophets and Sibyls after designs emanating from the Finiguerra-

Pollaiuolo workshop. The Otto prints and numerous other individual sheets in the style of this workshop were also his work.

Significantly enough, Baldini engraved two of the great early prints, the Judgment Hall of Pilate and the Conversion of Paul, designed by Sandro Botticelli. And much later — in 1481 — he engraved Botticelli's designs for an edition of Dante's *Divina Commedia*.

But Baldini was not Botticelli's preferred engraver. Botticelli found a more acceptable partner in Francesco Rosselli, a master who possibly from his work in the making of maps and charts, and surely in imitation of the technique used by Pollaiuolo for the Battle of the Naked Men, had developed a new style of engraving, the so-called broad manner. Nevertheless Botticelli's period of intense activity in collaboration with Rosselli, like that of Pollaiuolo with Finiguerra, was a limited one, ranging from about 1465 to 1470 or 1475. During that brief span, however, Botticelli was able to produce his versions of the Prophets and the Sibyls, and of the Triumphs of Petrarch. Meanwhile he also designed the completely new series of the Life of the Virgin and of Christ, as well as a number of notable single prints.

After about 1475 much of the vital spark seems to have faded from the Florentine school of engraving. By that time almost all the great prints had been made. Pollaiuolo had found more commanding interests, and so, too, had Botticelli. Thus it is that this account of the history of Florentine niello work and engraving (if we omit the few early nielli by Finiguerra) is encompassed within a brief fifteen years. Yet during that short period our five masters functioned with an almost inspired impulse.

The period's lasting greatness may be credited to those two extraordinary men, Pollaiuolo and Botticelli, who set standards that still remain golden. The tragedy is that no master of the first rank rose up to follow Botticelli, as Botticelli had followed Pollaiuolo. Those who continued to produce engravings were of the less gifted sort, like Baldini, who by his dedication to the engraver's art had made himself the Alinari of his day.

APPENDICES · REFERENCES · INDEX

APPENDICES

Appendix A. CHRONOLOGICAL LIST OF THE ENGRAVED WORKS BY FINIGUERRA, POLLAIUOLO, BALDINI, AND ROSSELLI THAT HAVE BEEN SPECIFICALLY MENTIONED IN THE TEXT

NOTE: *The following list does not presume to include all the works that may have been produced by this group of early Florentine designers and engravers.*

FINIGUERRA

About 1452–1455

Sulphur casts. After his own designs:

    The 7 plaques from the series of the Creation. Hind, *Nielli*, nos. 134–140.

    The 14 plaques from the series of the Passion. Hind, *Nielli*, nos. 142–150; Blum, *Les Nielles*, nos. 2–6.

Niello. After his own design:

    The Crucifixion pax. Hind, *Nielli*, plate II, C.

About 1459–1464

Niello prints. After designs made in collaboration with Pollaiuolo:

    Justice. Blum, *Les Nielles*, nos. 34 and 34 bis.

    The Madonna and Child Enthroned between Saint Stephen and Saint Alban. Blum, *Les Nielles*, no. 172.

    A Schoolmaster Surrounded by His Pupils. Blum, *Les Nielles*, no. 19.

    The Arming of Hector. Blum, *Les Nielles*, nos. 14 and 14 bis.

    Hector and Achilles. Blum, *Les Nielles*, no. 199.

    The Crucifixion. Blum, *Les Nielles*, no. 205.

    The Baptism of Christ. Blum, *Les Nielles*, nos. 25 and 25 bis.

    Seated Nude Youth. Blum, *Les Nielles*, no. 38.

    Cain and Abel. Blum, *Les Nielles*, no. 164.

    The Sacrifice of Abraham. Blum, *Les Nielles*, no. 11.

    The Beheading of a Captive. Blum, *Les Nielles*, nos. 35 and 35 bis.

Sulphur cast. After a design made in collaboration with Pollaiuolo:

    The Coronation of the Virgin. Hind, *Nielli*, no. 151.

About 1461–1462

Copperplate prints. After designs made in collaboration with Pollaiuolo:

    The 7 engravings of the first series of the Planets. Hind, *Early Italian Engraving*, A.III.1,a–7,a.

    The Triumph of Bacchus and Ariadne. Hind, A.II.26.

About 1461–1464

Copperplate prints. After designs made in collaboration with Pollaiuolo:
    The Procession to Calvary and the Crucifixion. Hind, A.II.8.
    The Beheading of a Captive. Hind, A.II.11.
    The Fight for the Hose. Hind, A.II.5.
    The King of the Goats. Hind, A.II.23.
    Saint Nicholas, Patron of Sailors. Hind, A.I.62.

POLLAIUOLO

About 1460–1462

Copperplate print. After his own design:
    The Battle of the Naked Men (The Dragon's Teeth). Hind, D.I.1.

BALDINI

About 1460–1461

Copperplate print. After his own design:
    The Resurrection with a Table to Find Easter, 1461. Hind, A.I.7.

About 1460–1463

Copperplate prints
  After nielli engraved by Finiguerra:
    The Baptism of Christ. Hind, A.I.10.
    The Coronation of the Virgin. Hind, A.I.12.
  After his own designs:
    A Gallant and His Mistress Holding a Crown. Hind, A.IV.19.
    Virgil the Sorcerer. Hind, A.I.47.
    The Death and Assumption of the Virgin. Hind, A.I.11.
    The Virgin and Child Enthroned between Saint Theodore and Saint Catherine. Hind, A.I.35.

About 1463–1464

Copperplate prints
  After a design by Finiguerra:
    The Triumph of Love, from the series of the Vienna Triumphs of Petrarch. Hind, A.I.18.
  After his own designs (?):
    5 of the 6 engravings of the Vienna Triumphs of Petrarch. Hind, A.I.19–23.
    The 10 engravings of the Vienna Passion. Hind, A.I.25–34.
  After an engraving by the Master of the Banderoles:
    The Mass of Saint Gregory. Hind, A.I.44.
  After a painting attributed to Orcagna:
    The Inferno According to Dante. Hind, A.I.60.

About 1464–1465

Nielli
  After designs made by Finiguerra in collaboration with Pollaiuolo:
    The 20 plaques on the Metropolitan Museum's cross. Hind, *Nielli*, p. 8, note 1.
  After a niello engraved by Finiguerra:
    The Crucifixion pax. Hind, *Nielli*, pl. I (A).

Copperplate prints. After engravings by Finiguerra:
    The 8 engravings of the second series of the Planets. Hind, A.III.1,b–8,b.
    The second Procession to Calvary and the Crucifixion. Hind, A.II.7.

About 1465–1475

Copperplate prints
  After designs by Botticelli:
    The Judgment Hall of Pilate. Hind, A.II.9.
    The Conversion of Paul. Hind, A.II.10.
    The plate of 8 border panels for the first series of the Planets. Hind, A.III.9,a.
  After designs from the Finiguerra-Pollaiuolo workshop:
    The Virgin and Child Standing before a Throne with Saint Sebastian and Saint Catherine. Hind, A.II.25.
    Saint Catherine of Siena. Hind, A.I.66.
    The 24 engravings of the first series of the Prophets. Hind, C.I.1,a–24,a.
    The 12 engravings of the first series of the Sibyls. Hind, C.II.1,a–12,a.
  After a painting by Domenico di Michelino:
    Dante as the Poet of the Divine Comedy. Hind, A.I.61.

About 1465–1480

Copperplate prints
  After drawings from Finiguerra's Picture-Chronicle:
    Judith with the Head of Holophernes. Hind, A.IV.1.
    Jason and Medea. Hind, A.IV.6.
    Woman with Unicorn. Hind, A.IV.4.
    The Cretan Labyrinth. Hind, A.II.16.
    Story of the Creation. Hind, A.II.1.
  After an earlier engraving by Baldini, and designs from the Finiguerra-Pollaiuolo workshop:
    The Inferno According to Dante. Hind, A.I.59.
    The 3 illustrations from the *Monte Sancto di Dio* (1477). Hind, A.V.1 (1–3).

About 1480–1487 (?)

Copperplate prints
  After designs by Botticelli:
    The 19 illustrations from the *Divina Commedia* with a commentary by Landino (1481). Hind, A.V.2 (1–19).
  After designs from unidentified sources:
    Christ on the Cross between the Virgin and Saint John. Hind, A.I.83.
    Tobias and the Angel. Hind, A.I.82.
    The Story of the Dead King and His Sons. Hind, A.I.52.

ROSSELLI

About 1465–1475

Copperplate prints. After designs by Botticelli:
    The 24 engravings in the second series of the Prophets. Hind, C.I.1,b–24,b.
    The 12 engravings in the second series of the Sibyls. Hind, C.II.1,b–12,b.

The 17 engravings in the series of the Life of the Virgin and of Christ, including two plates of
    border panels. Hind, B.I.1–17.
The 6 engravings in the series of the Triumphs of Petrarch. Hind, B.II.1–6.
David and Goliath. Hind, B.III.6.
The Adoration of the Magi. Hind, B.III.2.
The Deluge (2 versions). Hind, B.III.1 and 3.
Solomon and the Queen of Sheba. Hind, B.III.4.
Moses on Mount Sinai and the Brazen Serpent. Hind, B.III.5.

After 1475
Copperplate prints. After designs by Botticelli:
    The Last Supper. Hind, B.III.11.
    The Last Judgment. Hind, B.III.7.
    The Preaching of Fra Marco. Hind, B.III.8.
    The Virgin and Child Enthroned between Saint Helena and Saint Michael. Hind, B.III.9.
    The Assumption of the Virgin. Hind, B.III.10.

After 1480
Copperplate prints. After his own designs (?):
    View of Florence. Hind, B.III.18.
    Map of the World. Hind, G.6.

Appendix B. LIST OF OTHER WORKS BY FINIGUERRA THAT HAVE BEEN SPECIFICALLY MENTIONED IN THE TEXT

Designs for intarsias

1463–1464. Designs, executed under the supervision of Giuliano da Maiano, for intarsia panels in the
Sacristy of the Florentine Duomo
    In the style of Baldovinetti:
        Saint Zenobius Flanked by Two Deacons, Saint Eugene and Saint Crescentius.
        The Presentation in the Temple.
    Made in collaboration with Pollaiuolo:
        The Annunciation.
        Amos.
        Isaiah.

Drawings

Probably made in 1464
    The 107 drawings in the Florentine Picture-Chronicle.

REFERENCES CITED

Aiazzi, G. (ed.). *Ricordi storici di Filippo di Cino Rinuccini dal 1282 al 1460*. Florence, 1840.

Archivio di Stato, Florence. Carte Strozziane, series II, no. 51, entitled *Fatti e memorie dell'arte dei mercatanti:* Vol. I, Deliberationi de' Consoli, 1455–1459, carta 216, recto (February 22, 1457); Vol. I, Libro grande dell'arte de' mercatanti, marked E, 1459, carta 10; Vol. II, Ornamenti, carta 111, tergo.

—— Catasto, portate dell'anno 1457; quartiere di S. Maria Novella, gonfalone Unicorno; no. 813, no. 163.

—— Magistrato dei Pupilli avanti il Principato, file no. 190, entitled "Filze e inventari di Firenze dall'anno 1526 al 1529," no. 52.

Bandinelli, Baccio. Letter. In G. Bottari (& Stefano Ticozzi), *Raccolta di lettere*, Vol. I, pp. 104 f. Milan, 1822.

Bartsch, Adam. *Le Peintre Graveur*. Vienna, 1803–1821.

Berenson, Bernard. *The Drawings of the Florentine Painters*. 3 vols. Chicago: University of Chicago Press, 1938.

—— *The Florentine Painters of the Renaissance*. Third edition. New York and London: G. P. Putnam's Sons, 1909.

Blum, André. *Les Nielles du quattrocento* (Musée du Louvre, Cabinet des Estampes Edmond de Rothschild). Paris: Compagnie des Arts Photomécaniques, 1950.

Bunt, Cyril G. E. "A Florentine Nielloed Cross," *Burlington Magazine*, LXV (1934), pp. 26 ff.

Colvin, Sidney. *A Florentine Picture-Chronicle*. London: Bernard Quaritch, 1898.

Dutuit, Eugène. *Manuel de l'amateur d'estampes, Nielles*. Paris: A. Lévy; London: Delau et Cie. Vol. I, Part II, 1888.

Essling, Prince d'. *Les Livres à figures vénitiens*. Florence: Leo S. Olschki; Paris: Henri Leclerc. Part I, Vol. I, 1907.

—— *Les Missels imprimés à Venise de 1481 à 1600*. Paris: J. Rothschild, 1896.

Filarete, Antonio Averlino. *Trattato d'architettura*. In Michele Lazzaroni and Antonio Muñoz (ed.), *Filarete*. Rome, 1908.

Hind, Arthur M. *Early Italian Engraving*. 7 vols. London: Bernard Quaritch, Ltd., 1938–1948.

—— *Nielli*. London: British Museum, 1936.

Kennedy, Ruth Wedgwood. *Alesso Baldovinetti*. New Haven: Yale University Press, 1938.

Kristeller, Paul. "Die italienischen Niellodrucke und der Kupferstich des XV Jahrhundert," *Jahrbuch der Königlichen Preussischen Kunstsammlungen*, XV (1894), p. 115.

Kunstsammlung Karl Thewalt, Köln (Lempertz sale). Cologne, 1903.

Lanzi, Luigi. *Storia pittorica della Italia*. Ed. 1809. Vol. I, p. 90.

Lehrs, Max. *Geschichte und kritischer Katalog des deutschen, niederlandischen und französischen Kupferstichs im XV Jahrhundert*. Vienna: Gesellschaft für Vervielfältigende Kunst. Vol. I, 1908; Vol. IV, 1921.

Maclagan, Eric, and Longhurst, Margaret H. *Catalogue of Italian Sculpture*. London: Victoria and
    Albert Museum, 1932.

Ortolani, Sergio. *Il Pollaiuolo*. Milan: Ulrico Hoepli, 1948.

Panofsky, Erwin. *Albrecht Dürer*. 2 vols. Princeton: Princeton University Press, 1948.

Pittaluga, Mary. *Filippo Lippi*. Florence: Del Turco, 1949.

Popham, A. E., and Pouncey, Philip. *Italian Drawings*. 2 vols. London: British Museum, 1950.

Rosenberg, Marc. *Niello* (Geschichte der Goldschmiedekunst). Frankfurt am Main: Joseph Baer
    & Co., 1925.

Sabatini, Attilio. *Antonio e Piero del Pollaiuolo*. Florence: G. C. Sansoni, 1944.

Venturi, Adolfo. *Botticelli*. Paris: G. Crès & Cie., 1926.

—— "La Pittura bolognese nel secolo XV," *Archivio storico dell'arte*, Vol. III, p. 287. Rome, 1891.

Walker, John. "Ricostruzione d'un'incisione Pollajolesca," *Dedalo*, Anno XIII, Vol. I (1933),
    pp. 229–237.

Passages from Cellini and Vasari that have been translated in the text were freely adapted from
the renderings by C. R. Ashbee, *The Treatises of Benvenuto Cellini on Goldsmithing and Sculpture* (London:
Kelmscott Press, 1898) and Gaston DuC. DeVere, *Lives of the Most Eminent Painters, Sculptors, and
Architects by Giorgio Vasari* (London: Philip Lee Warner, 1912–1914).

INDEX

Titles of works of art are indexed individually; they are not entered under the respective artists. Allusive references are given in quotation marks, usually after the page number.

Works bearing the same title are distinguished by medium or medium and artist.

Abbreviations for media of works of art are used as follows:

c p	copperplate print	n	niello
dr	drawing	n p	niello print
int	intarsia	s c	sulphur cast

PLATES

References to related Sections and Parts of the text are noted on Plates 2–112. Roman numbers indicate Sections, arabic numbers indicate Parts.

PHOTOGRAPHIC CREDITS

The sources of the reproductions are listed, for convenience in reference, under the names of the institutions and collections which own or lately owned the works represented in the plates.

In the entries below an asterisk (*) signifies: Negatives, Museum of Fine Arts, Boston — *at present deposited in the British Museum.*

Albertina, Vienna:

Plate 39 A, from Bernard Berenson, *The Drawings of the Florentine Painters* (University of Chicago Press, Chicago: 1938), cat. no. 1909, Vol. III, fig. 73

Plates 48 B, 49 B, 75 B, 77 B, 79, 82, from photographs* courtesy of the British Museum

Plates 61, 76 B, 78 B, 89, from photographs courtesy of the Albertina

Plates 67, 95, from photographs copyrighted by the Museum of Fine Arts, Boston

Anonymous collection, Saaz:

Plate 68, from Arthur M. Hind, *Early Italian Engraving* (Bernard Quaritch Ltd., London: 1938), pl. 12*

Art Institute of Chicago:

Plate 91, from a photograph courtesy of the Art Institute of Chicago

Baptistry, Florence:

Plates 2 B, 3 B, 19 B, 20, 41 A, 42 A, 43 A, 44 B, 50 A, 94, from photographs by G. Brogi

Bargello, Florence:

Plates 7 B, 9, 32 B, 33, 84 A, from photographs by Cav. Nicolò Cipriani supplied by the Soprintendenza alle Gallerie, Florence

Bibliothèque Nationale, Paris:

Plates 71 A, 72, 73 B, 86 A, 98 B, from photographs copyrighted by the Museum of Fine Arts, Boston

British Museum, London:

By permission of the Trustees of the British Museum: Plates 1, 2 A, 3 A, 5 A, 7 A, 17, 41 B, 42 B, 43 B, 44 A, 45 B, 46 B, 47 B, 48 A, 49 A, 50 C, 51 B, 57, 58 A, 59, 60 A, 60 B, 62 A, 63, 70 A, 83, 84 B, 90, 92, 93, 96, 97 A, 100, 107, from photographs by John Freeman and Co.

Plates 56 B, 64, 87 A, 98 A, from photographs copyrighted by the Museum of Fine Arts, Boston

Plates 56 D, 86 B, 101, 102 A, 103 B, 104 A, 109 A, 111 B, from photographs* from an anonymous lender

Plate 62 B, from Sidney Colvin, *A Florentine Picture-Chronicle* (Bernard Quaritch, London: 1898), pl. 4

Plates 81, 87 B, 99, from photographs* courtesy of the British Museum

Plates 104 B, 110 B, 112 B, from Arthur M. Hind, *Early Italian Engraving* (Bernard Quaritch Ltd., London: 1938), pl. 191*

Duomo, Florence:

Plates 36, 37, 38, 39 B, 40 B, 50 B, from photographs by Cav. Nicolò Cipriani supplied by the Soprintendenza alle Gallerie, Florence

Duomo, Prato:

Plate 5 B, from a photograph by Alinari

Plate 110 A, from a photograph by Cav. Nicolò Cipriani supplied by the Soprintendenza alle Gallerie, Florence

Graphische Sammlung, Munich:

Plate 66 A, from a photograph courtesy of the Graphische Sammlung, Munich

Plate 71 B, from a photograph copyrighted by the Museum of Fine Arts, Boston

Hospital of Santa Maria Nuova, Florence:

Plate 88, from a photograph by Alinari

Kaiser Friedrich Museum, Berlin:

Plate 6, from a photograph by Berlin Photographie Gesellschaft

Plates 31 A, 66 B, 73 A, 73 C, 75 A, 76 A, 77 A, 78 A, from photographs courtesy of the Hessische Treuhandverwaltung

Kunsthalle, Hamburg:

Plates 65, 69, 105 A, from photographs copyrighted by the Kleinhempel Fotowerkstätten, Hamburg

Louvre, Paris:

Plates 4 A, 11 A, 11 B, 12 A, 12 B, 13 B, 14 A, 14 B, 15, 16, 18, 19 A, 19 C, 21, 51 A, 58 B, from photographs by the Compagnie des Arts Photomécaniques for André Blum, *Les Nielles du quattrocento* (Compagnie des Arts Photomécaniques, Paris: 1950)

Plates 102 B, 105 B, from a photograph by the Compagnie des Arts Photomécaniques for *Dessins et gravures du quattrocento*, a forthcoming work by André Blum

Metropolitan Museum of Art, New York:

Plates 4 B, 22, 23, 24, 25 A, 25 B, 26 A, 27 A, 28, 29 A, 29 B, 30 A, 30 B, 31 B, 32 A, 45 A, 46 A, 47 A, 52, 53 A, 54, 55 A, 55 B, 56 A, 56 C, 103 A, from photographs by Edward J. Milla and Thomas McAdams

Musée des Beaux-Arts, Budapest:

Plate 70 B, from Arthur M. Hind, *Early Italian Engraving* (Bernard Quaritch Ltd., London: 1938), pl. 147*

Museo dell'Opera del Duomo, Florence:

Plates 10, 26 B, 27 B, 35 A, 40 A, from photographs by Cav. Nicolò Cipriani supplied by the Soprintendenza alle Gallerie, Florence

Plate 34, from a photograph by Alinari

Museum, Prato:

Plate 111 A, from a photograph by Cav. Nicolò Cipriani supplied by the Soprintendenza alle Gallerie, Florence

Museum of Fine Arts, Boston:

Plates 85, 106, from photographs courtesy of the Museum of Fine Arts, Boston

San Lorenzo, Florence:

Plate 108, from a photograph by Cav. Nicolò Cipriani supplied by the Soprintendenza alle Gallerie, Florence

Seraglio Library, Istanbul:

Plate 80, from Arthur M. Hind, *Early Italian Engraving* (Bernard Quaritch Ltd., London: 1938), pl. 43*

Società Colombaria, Florence:

Plate 112 A, from a photograph by Cav. Nicolò Cipriani supplied by the Soprintendenza alle Gallerie, Florence

Uffizi, Florence:

Plates 13 A, 35 B, 109 B, from photographs by Cav. Nicolò Cipriani supplied by the Soprintendenza alle Gallerie, Florence

Plate 53 B, from a photograph by Alinari

Vatican Library, Rome:

Plate 97 B, from a photograph courtesy of the Vatican Library

Victoria and Albert Museum, London:

Plate 8, from a photograph, Crown copyrighted, courtesy of the Victoria and Albert Museum

Zwinger, Dresden:

Plate 71 C, from a photograph copyrighted by the Museum of Fine Arts, Boston

Location unknown:

Plate 74, from Arthur M. Hind, *Early Italian Engraving* (Bernard Quaritch Ltd., London: 1938), pl. 35*

View of a Goldsmith's Shop. Detail from the copperplate engraving of the Planet Mercury. Executed by Finiguerra after a design made in collaboration with Pollaiuolo. About 1461–1462. British Museum, London. Enlarged.

A

B

A. The Creation of Eve. Sulphur cast of a niello plaque. Engraved by Finiguerra about 1452–1455. British Museum, London. Reproduced in reverse. Enlarged. · B. The Creation of Eve. Detail from a bronze relief on Ghiberti's second Baptistry doors, which were set in place in 1452. Baptistry, Florence.

A

B

A. The Creation of Adam. Sulphur cast of a niello plaque. Engraved by Finiguerra about 1452–1455. British Museum, London. Reproduced in reverse. Enlarged. · B. The Creation of Adam. Detail from a bronze relief on Ghiberti's second Baptistry doors, which were set in place in 1452. Baptistry, Florence.

4

A

B

A. The Agony in the Garden. Sulphur cast of a niello plaque. Engraved by Finiguerra about 1452–1455. Louvre (Rothschild collection), Paris. Enlarged. · B. The Agony in the Garden. Woodcut illustration from Bonaventura, *Meditationi sopra la Passione*. Printed in Venice in 1487 from the blocks used in the Venetian block book *Passion of Our Lord* of about 1450. Metropolitan Museum, New York.

I · NIELLI · 2

opposite:
A. The Ascension. Sulphur cast of a niello plaque. Engraved by Finiguerra about 1452–1455. British Museum, London. Enlarged. · B. Christ in a Mandorla. Detail from the painting of the Burial of Saint Jerome. Executed by Fra Filippo Lippi (with the help of Fra Diamante) for the Duomo at Prato about 1453.

A

B

6

Three Women. Detail from the Miracle of Saint Ambrose. Painted by Fra Filippo Lippi
in the 1440s. Kaiser Friedrich Museum, Berlin.

I · NIELLI · 2

A   B

A. The Resurrection, and the Three Marys at the Tomb. Sulphur cast of a niello plaque.
Engraved by Finiguerra about 1452–1455. British Museum, London. Enlarged. · B. Group
at the Foot of the Cross. Detail from the niello pax of the Crucifixion (Plate 9).
Engraved by Finiguerra about 1452–1455.

I · NIELLI · 2

8

The Crucifixion. Terracotta relief. Presumably after a design made by Ghiberti about 1440–1450. Victoria and Albert Museum, London.

I · NIELLI · 2

The Crucifixion. Niello pax. Engraved by Finiguerra for the Florentine Baptistry about 1452–1455. Bargello, Florence. Enlarged.

I · NIELLI · 2

Moses. Repoussé silver plaque (originally enameled) decorating a cross made for the Baptistry of Florence. Executed by Pollaiuolo between 1457 and 1459. Museo dell'Opera del Duomo, Florence.

I · NIELLI · 3

opposite:
A. Justice. Niello print. Engraved by Finiguerra after a design made in collaboration with Pollaiuolo. About 1459–1464. Louvre (Rothschild collection), Paris. Reproduced in reverse. Enlarged. · B. The Madonna and Child Enthroned between Saint Stephen and Saint Alban. Niello print. Engraved by Finiguerra after a design made in collaboration with Pollaiuolo. About 1459–1464. Louvre (Rothschild collection), Paris. Enlarged.

A

B

A

B

A. A Schoolmaster Surrounded by His Pupils. Niello print. Engraved by Finiguerra
after a design made in collaboration with Pollaiuolo. About 1459–1464. Louvre
(Rothschild collection), Paris. Enlarged. · B. The Arming of Hector. Niello print.
Engraved by Finiguerra after a design made in collaboration with Pollaiuolo. About
1459–1464. Louvre (Rothschild collection), Paris. Enlarged.

A

B

A. An Angel. Detail from the altarpiece of the Coronation of the Virgin. Painted in the 1440s by Fra Filippo Lippi. Uffizi, Florence. · B. Kneeling Girl. Detail from the niello print of the Arming of Hector (Plate 12. B).

A   B

A. Hector and Achilles. Niello print. Engraved by Finiguerra after a design made in collaboration with Pollaiuolo. About 1459–1464. Louvre (Rothschild collection), Paris. Enlarged. · B. Roman Soldiers. Detail from the niello print of the Crucifixion (Plate 16).

The Swooning Virgin. Detail from the niello print of the Crucifixion (Plate 16).

16

The Crucifixion. Niello print of a pax made for the Florentine Baptistry. Engraved by
Finiguerra after a design made in collaboration with Pollaiuolo. About 1459–1464.
Louvre (Rothschild collection), Paris. Enlarged.

I · NIELLI · 3

The Coronation of the Virgin. Sulphur cast of a pax. Engraved by Finiguerra after a design made in collaboration with Pollaiuolo. About 1459–1464. British Museum, London. Enlarged.

I · NIELLI · 3

The Baptism of Christ. Niello print. Engraved by Finiguerra after a design made in collaboration with Pollaiuolo. About 1459–1464. Louvre (Rothschild collection), Paris. Enlarged.

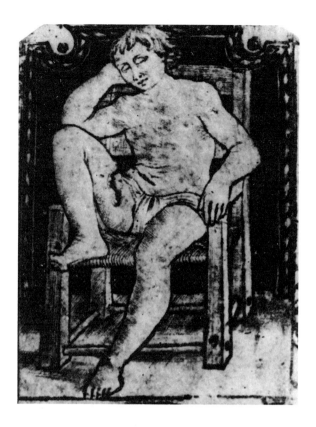

A. Seated Nude Youth. Niello print. Engraved by Finiguerra after a design made in collaboration with Pollaiuolo. About 1459–1464. Louvre (Rothschild collection), Paris. Enlarged.

B

C

B. Cain and Abel. Detail from a bronze relief on Ghiberti's second Baptistry doors, which were set in place in 1452. Baptistry, Florence. · C. Cain and Abel. Niello print. Engraved by Finiguerra after a design made in collaboration with Pollaiuolo. About 1459–1464. Louvre (Rothschild collection), Paris. Reproduced in reverse. Enlarged.

The Sacrifice of Abraham. Detail from a bronze relief on Ghiberti's second Baptistry doors, which were set in place in 1452. Baptistry, Florence.

I · NIELLI · 3

The Sacrifice of Abraham. Niello print. Engraved by Finiguerra after a design made in collaboration with Pollaiuolo. About 1459–1464. Louvre (Rothschild collection), Paris. Enlarged.

I · NIELLI · 3

The front of a silver-gilt cross decorated with niello plaques. Engraved by Baldini for a convent of the Poor Clares in Florence, about 1464–1465. Metropolitan Museum, New York; gift of J. Pierpont Morgan, 1917. Width across arms 32 cm.

I · NIELLI · 4

The back of the Metropolitan Museum's cross, decorated with niello plaques engraved by Baldini. (Nine of the twenty plaques on the cross are illustrated in the succeeding plates.)

I · NIELLI · 4

Christ Crucified. Niello plaque from the Metropolitan Museum's cross (Plate 23). Engraved by Baldini after a design by Finiguerra in collaboration with Pollaiuolo. Enlarged.

I · NIELLI · 4

A. The Flagellation. Niello plaque from the Metropolitan Museum's cross (Plate 23). Engraved by Baldini after a design by Finiguerra in collaboration with Pollaiuolo. Enlarged. · B. The Crowning with Thorns. Niello plaque from the Metropolitan Museum's cross (Plate 23). Engraved by Baldini after a design by Finiguerra in collaboration with Pollaiuolo. Enlarged.

26

A. The Mourning Virgin. Niello plaque from the Metropolitan Museum's cross (Plate 22). Engraved by Baldini after a design by Finiguerra in collaboration with Pollaiuolo. Enlarged. · B. Faith. Repousse silver plaque (originally enameled), decorating a cross made for the Baptistry of Florence. Executed by Pollaiuolo between 1457 and 1459. Museo dell'Opera del Duomo, Florence.

A. Saint Mary Magdalen. Niello plaque from the Metropolitan Museum's cross (Plate 22). Engraved by Baldini after a design by Finiguerra in collaboration with Pollaiuolo. Enlarged. · B. Standing Woman. Detail from the embroidered panel of Zacharias Writing the Name of the Baptist, one of a series that Pollaiuolo was commissioned in 1466 to produce for the Baptistry of Florence.

I · NIELLI · 4

28

Saint John. Niello plaque from the Metropolitan Museum's cross (Plate 22). Engraved
by Baldini after a design by Finiguerra in collaboration with Pollaiuolo. Enlarged.

I · NIELLI · 4

A

B

A. The Agony in the Garden. Niello plaque from the Metropolitan Museum's cross (Plate 22). Engraved by Baldini after a design by Finiguerra. Enlarged. · B. Pietà. Niello plaque from the Metropolitan Museum's cross (Plate 23). Engraved by Baldini after a design by Finiguerra in collaboration with Pollaiuolo. Enlarged.

I · NIELLI · 4

A

B

A. The Last Supper. Niello plaque from the Metropolitan Museum's cross (Plate 23).
Engraved by Baldini after a design by Finiguerra. Enlarged. · B. Detail showing Baldini's
cypher, from the niello plaque of The Last Supper (Plate 30 A). Enlarged.

A

B

A. The Last Supper. Detail from a woodcut illustration from the block book *Passion of Our Lord*. Printed in Venice about 1450. Kaiser Friedrich Museum, Berlin. · B. Detail from the niello plaque of The Last Supper (Plate 30 A). Enlarged.

I · NIELLI · 4

A   B

A. Saint John. Detail from a niello plaque from the Metropolitan Museum's cross (Plate 28). Engraved by Baldini. Enlarged. · B. Head of a Young Man. Detail from a niello pax of the Crucifixion in the Bargello (Plate 33). Engraved by Baldini. Enlarged.

The Crucifixion. Niello pax. Engraved by Baldini about 1464–1465 as a variant of a pax engraved by Finiguerra (Plate 16). Bargello, Florence. Enlarged.

I · NIELLI · 4

Saint Zenobius Flanked by Two Deacons, Saint Eugene and Saint Crescentius. Intarsia panel. Designed by Finiguerra and executed under the supervision of Giuliano da Maiano. 1463–1464. Museo dell'Opera del Duomo, Florence.

II · INTARSIAS · 2

B

A

A. Saint Eugene or Saint Crescentius. Detail from the intarsia panel of Saint Zenobius (Plate 34) designed by Finiguerra. · B. Saint Lawrence. Detail from the Cafaggiolo altarpiece. Painted by Baldovinetti about 1454. Uffizi, Florence.

II · INTARSIAS · 2

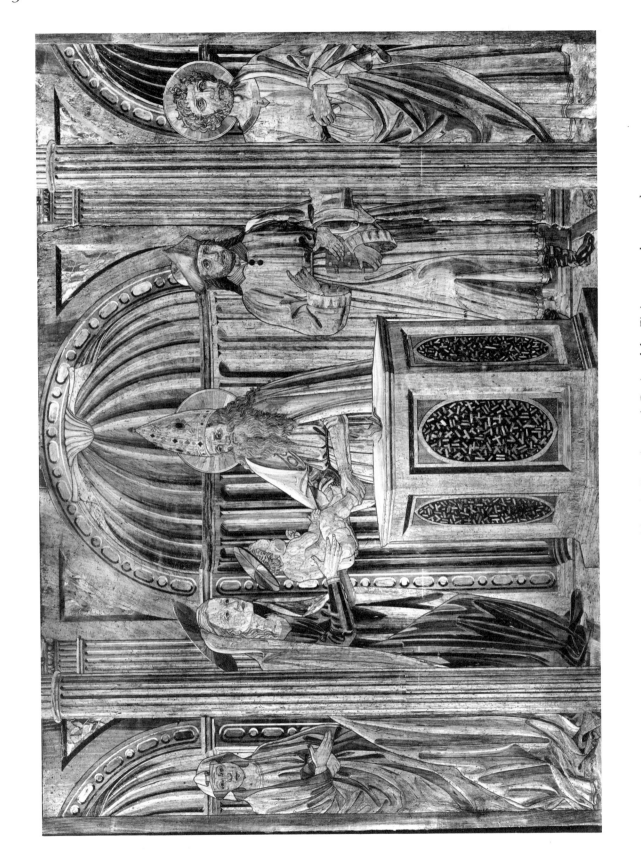

The Presentation in the Temple. Intarsia panel. Designed by Finiguerra and executed under the supervision of Giuliano da Maiano. 1463–1464. Sacristy of the Duomo, Florence.

II · INTARSIAS · 2

The Annunciation. Intarsia panel. Designed by Finiguerra in collaboration with Pollaiuolo, and executed under the supervision of Giuliano da Maiano. 1463–1464. Sacristy of the Duomo, Florence.

II · INTARSIAS · 2

Amos. Intarsia panel. Designed by Finiguerra in collaboration with Pollaiuolo, and executed under the supervision of Giuliano da Maiano. 1463–1464. Sacristy of the Duomo, Florence.

II · INTARSIAS · 2

A

B

A. Man Standing. Detail from Two Men Conversing. Presumably drawn by Pollaiuolo.
Albertina, Vienna. · B. Isaiah. Intarsia panel. Designed by Finiguerra in collaboration
with Pollaiuolo, and executed under the supervision of Giuliano da Maiano. 1463–1464.
Sacristy of the Duomo, Florence.

II · INTARSIAS · 2

A

B

A. Head of Saint Eugene or Saint Crescentius. Detail from the intarsia panel of Saint Zenobius (Plate 34) designed by Finiguerra. · B. Head of the Prophet Amos. Detail from the intarsia panel (Plate 38) designed by Finiguerra in collaboration with Pollaiuolo.

A

B

A. Samson. Detail from the bronze enframement on Ghiberti's second Baptistry doors, which were set in place in 1452. Baptistry, Florence. · B. Adam. Detail from the Picture-Chronicle. Drawn by Finiguerra, probably in 1464. British Museum, London. Enlarged.

A

B

A. A Prophet. Detail from the bronze enframement on Ghiberti's second Baptistry doors, which were set in place in 1452. Baptistry, Florence. · B. Samuel. Detail from the Picture-Chronicle. Drawn by Finiguerra, probably in 1464. British Museum, London. Reduced.

III · DRAWINGS · 2

A

B

A. Joshua. Detail from a bronze relief on Ghiberti's second Baptistry doors, which were set in place in 1452. Baptistry, Florence. · B. Minos. Detail from the Picture-Chronicle. Drawn by Finiguerra, probably in 1464. British Museum, London. Reduced.

A

B

A. Moses Receiving the Tables of the Law. Detail from the Picture-Chronicle. Drawn by Finiguerra, probably in 1464. British Museum, London. Reduced. · B. Moses Receiving the Tables of the Law. Detail from a bronze relief on Ghiberti's second Baptistry doors, which were set in place in 1452. Baptistry, Florence.

A. The Agony in the Garden. Niello plaque from the Metropolitan Museum's cross (Plate 22). Designed by Finiguerra. Enlarged. · B. The Death of Aeschylus. Detail from the Florentine Picture-Chronicle. Drawn by Finiguerra, probably in 1464. British Museum, London. Reduced.

III · DRAWINGS · 2

B

A

A. *Warriors.* Detail from Pollaiuolo's Battle of the Naked Men (Plate 52). About 1460–1462. Reduced. · B. *Cain.* Detail from
the Picture-Chronicle. Drawn by Finiguerra, probably in 1464. British Museum, London. Reproduced in reverse. Reduced.

III · DRAWINGS · 2

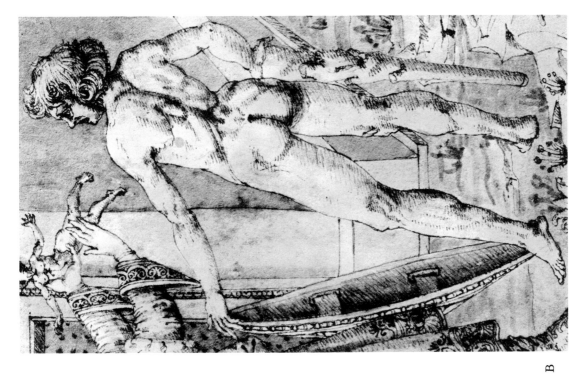

B

A

A. Warriors. Detail from Pollaiuolo's Battle of the Naked Men (Plate 52). About 1460–1462. Reduced. · B. Nude Male Figure.
Detail from the Picture-Chronicle. Drawn by Finiguerra, probably in 1464. British Museum, London. About actual size.

III · DRAWINGS · 2

48

A

B

A. Talthybius. Detail from the Picture-Chronicle. Drawn by Finiguerra, probably in 1464. British Museum, London. Reduced. · B. Personage. Detail from the copperplate engraving of the Triumph of Love (Plate 82). Designed by Finiguerra and engraved by Baldini. About 1463–1464. Albertina, Vienna. Enlarged.

III · DRAWINGS · 2

A

B

A. Helen and Paris. Detail from the Picture-Chronicle. Drawn by Finiguerra, probably in 1464. British Museum, London. Reduced. · B. Personage. Detail from the copperplate engraving of the Triumph of Love (Plate 82). Designed by Finiguerra and engraved by Baldini. About 1463–1464. Albertina, Vienna. Enlarged.

III · DRAWINGS · 2

50

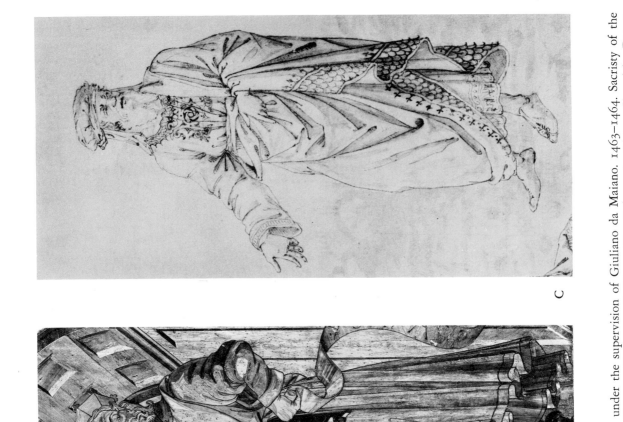

C

B

A

A. A Prophet. Detail from the bronze enframement on Ghiberti's second Baptistry doors (1452). Baptistry, Florence. · B. Isaiah. Intarsia panel. Designed by Finiguerra in collaboration with Pollaiuolo, and executed under the supervision of Giuliano da Maiano. 1463–1464. Sacristy of the Duomo, Florence. · C. Hosea. Detail from the Picture-Chronicle. Drawn by Finiguerra, probably in 1464. British Museum, London. Reduced.

III · DRAWINGS · 2

52

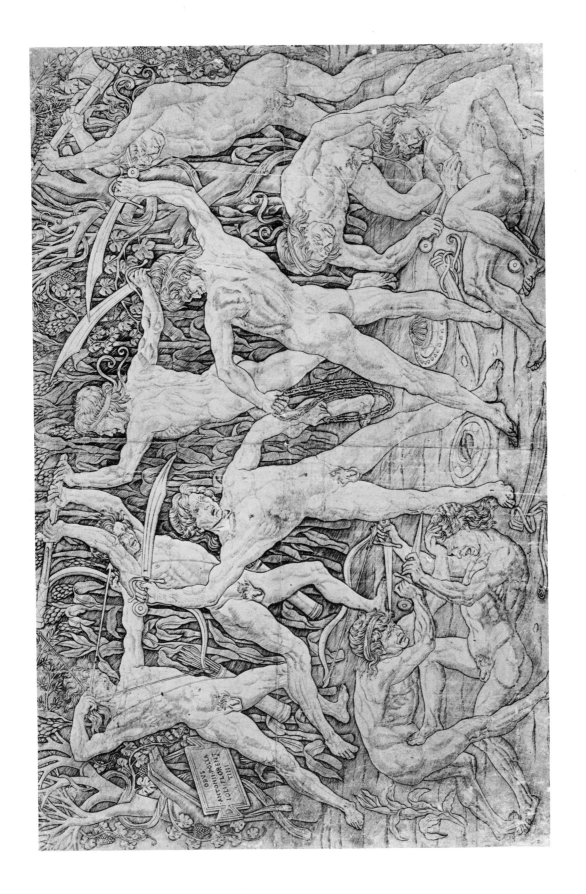

The Battle of the Naked Men (The Dragon's Teeth). Copperplate engraving. Designed and executed by Pollaiuolo about 1460–1462. Metropolitan Museum, New York. Reduced.

IV · COPPERPLATE ENGRAVINGS · 2

B

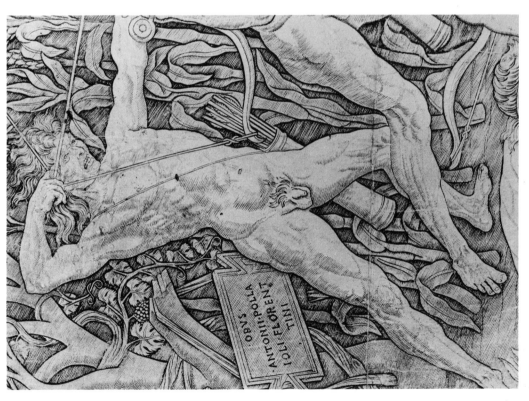

A

A. Bowman. Detail from Pollaiuolo's Battle of the Naked Men (Plate 52). About 1460–1462. Reduced. · B. Hercules and the Hydra. Painted by Pollaiuolo. Uffizi, Florence.

IV · COPPERPLATE ENGRAVINGS · 2

Hercules and the Giants. Copperplate engraving. Designed by a late follower of Pollaiuolo, and executed by a North Italian master of the school of Mantegna about 1500. Metropolitan Museum, New York. Reduced.

IV · COPPERPLATE ENGRAVINGS · 2

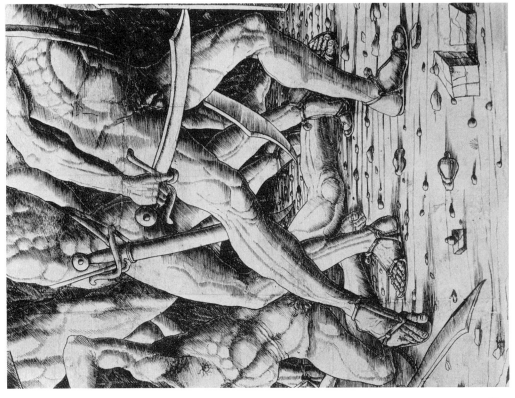

OPVS
ANTONII POLLA
IOLI FLOREN
TINI

A. Detail from Pollaiuolo's Battle of the Naked Men (Plate 52). About 1460–1462. Reduced. · B. Detail from the engraving of Hercules and the Giants (Plate 54). Executed by a North Italian master about 1500. Reduced.

IV · COPPERPLATE ENGRAVINGS · 2

56

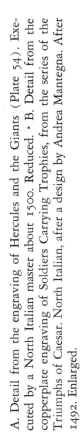

B

A

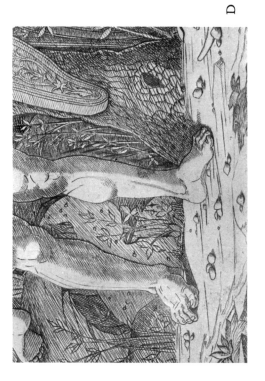

D

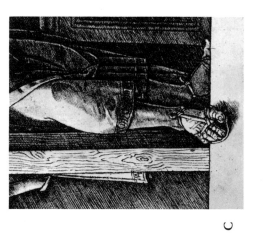

C

A. Detail from the engraving of Hercules and the Giants (Plate 54). Executed by a North Italian master about 1500. Reduced. · B. Detail from the copperplate engraving of Soldiers Carrying Trophies, from the series of the Triumphs of Caesar. North Italian, after a design by Andrea Mantegna. After 1492. Enlarged.

C. Detail from Mantegna's copperplate engraving of the Risen Christ between Saint Andrew and Saint Longinus. Probably about 1500. Metropolitan Museum, New York. Reduced. · D. Detail from the copperplate engraving of Hercules and Antaeus. Executed by Nicoletto Rosex da Modena, probably about 1500. British Museum, London. Reduced.

IV · COPPERPLATE ENGRAVINGS · 2

Combat Scene. Detail from the copperplate engraving of the Planet Mars. Executed by Finiguerra after a design made in collaboration with Pollaiuolo. About 1461–1462. British Museum, London. Enlarged.

IV · COPPERPLATE ENGRAVINGS · 3

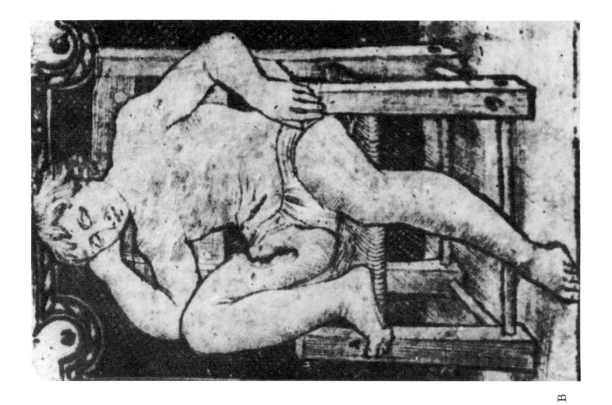

B

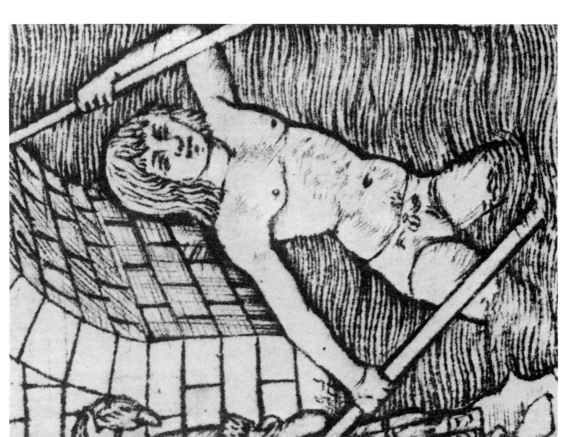

A

A. Boy Fishing. Detail from the copperplate engraving of the Planet Moon (see also Plate 59). Executed by Finiguerra after a design made in collaboration with Pollaiuolo. About 1461–1462. Enlarged. · B. Seated Nude Youth. Niello print. Engraved by Finiguerra after a design made in collaboration with Pollaiuolo. About 1459–1464. Louvre (Rothschild collection), Paris. Enlarged.

IV · COPPERPLATE ENGRAVINGS · 3

Boys Fishing and Swimming. Detail from the copperplate engraving of the Planet Moon. Executed by Finiguerra after a design made in collaboration with Pollaiuolo. About 1461–1462. British Museum, London. Enlarged.

IV · COPPERPLATE ENGRAVINGS · 3

B

A

A. Gymnasts. Detail from the copperplate engraving of the Planet Sun. Executed by Finiguerra after a design made in collaboration with Pollaiuolo. About 1461–1462. British Museum, London. Reduced. · B. Bathing Scene. Detail from the copperplate engraving of the Planet Venus. Executed by Finiguerra after a design made in collaboration with Pollaiuolo. About 1461–1462. British Museum, London. Enlarged.

IV · COPPERPLATE ENGRAVINGS · 3

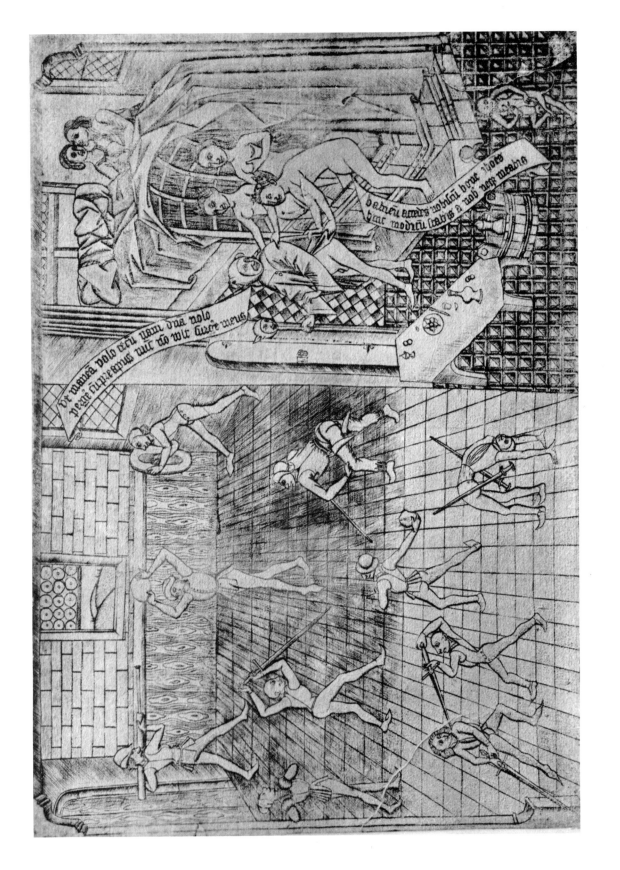

A Tilting Gallery and a Bathing Scene. Copperplate engraving. Executed by the Master of the Banderoles. Albertina, Vienna. Reduced.

IV · COPPERPLATE ENGRAVINGS · 3

62

B

A

A. Girl with a Flail. Detail from the copperplate engraving of the Planet Saturn. Executed by Finiguerra after a design made in collaboration with Pollaiuolo. About 1461–1462. British Museum, London. Reproduced in reverse. Enlarged. · B. A Grape-vine. Detail from the Picture-Chronicle. Drawn by Finiguerra, probably in 1464. British Museum, London. About actual size.

IV · COPPERPLATE ENGRAVINGS · 3

The Triumph of Bacchus and Ariadne. The left panel of two copperplate engravings. Executed by Finiguerra after a design made in collaboration with Pollaiuolo. About 1461–1462. British Museum, London. Reduced.

IV · COPPERPLATE ENGRAVINGS · 3

64

The Procession to Calvary and the Crucifixion. Copperplate engraving. Executed by
Finiguerra after a design made in collaboration with Pollaiuolo. About 1461–1464. British
Museum, London. Reduced.

The Beheading of a Captive. Copperplate engraving. Executed by Finiguerra after a design made in collaboration with Pollaiuolo. About 1461–1464. Kunsthalle, Hamburg. Reduced.

IV · COPPERPLATE ENGRAVINGS · 3

A

B

A. The Fight for the Hose. Copperplate engraving. Executed by Finiguerra after a design made in collaboration with Pollaiuolo. About 1461–1464. Graphische Sammlung, Munich. Reduced. · B. The Fight for the Hose. Copperplate engraving. Executed by the Master of the Banderoles. Kaiser Friedrich Museum, Berlin. Reduced.

IV · COPPERPLATE ENGRAVINGS · 3

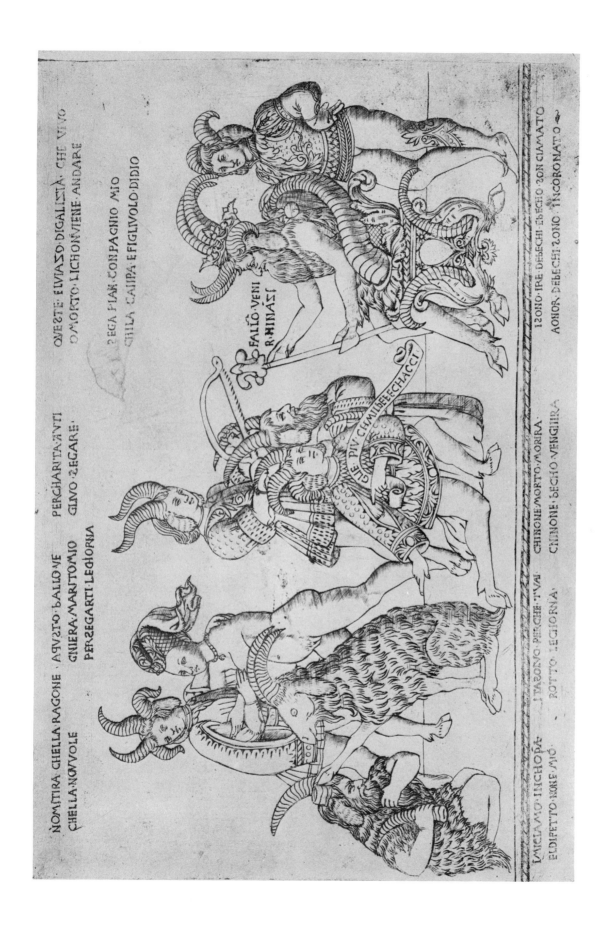

67

The King of the Goats. Copperplate engraving. Executed by Finiguerra after a design made in collaboration with Pollaiuolo. About 1461–1464. Albertina, Vienna. Reduced.

IV · COPPERPLATE ENGRAVINGS · 3

68

The Coronation of the Virgin. Copperplate engraving. Executed by Baldini after a design
made by Finiguerra in collaboration with Pollaiuolo (see Plate 17). About 1460–1463.
Anonymous collection, Saaz. Reduced.

The Baptism of Christ. Copperplate engraving. Executed by Baldini after a design by Finiguerra in collaboration with Pollaiuolo (see Plate 18). About 1460–1463. Kunsthalle, Hamburg. Reduced.

IV · COPPERPLATE ENGRAVINGS · 4, 5

A. Detail from the copperplate engraving of the Resurrection with a Table to Find
Easter, 1461. Designed and executed by Baldini, 1460–1461. British Museum, London.
Reduced. · B. A Gallant and His Mistress Holding a Crown. Copperplate engraving.
Designed and executed by Baldini about 1460–1463. Musée des Beaux-Arts, Budapest.
Reduced.

IV · COPPERPLATE ENGRAVINGS · 4, 5

A. Adam and Eve. Copperplate engraving. Executed by the Master of the Banderoles. Bibliothèque Nationale, Paris. Enlarged.

B

C

B. Nude Woman with a Rose. Copperplate engraving. Executed by the Master of the Banderoles. Graphische Sammlung, Munich. Reduced. · C. Febilla. Detail from the copperplate engraving of Virgil the Sorcerer. Designed and executed by Baldini about 1460–1463. Zwinger, Dresden. Reduced.

IV · COPPERPLATE ENGRAVINGS · 4, 5

The Death and Assumption of the Virgin. Copperplate engraving. Designed and executed by Baldini about 1460–1463. Bibliothèque Nationale, Paris. Reduced.

IV · COPPERPLATE ENGRAVINGS · 4, 5

C

B

A

A. Saint Simon. Copperplate engraving. Executed by the Master of the Year 1446. Kaiser Friedrich Museum, Berlin. About actual size. · B. The Death of the Virgin. Detail from Baldini's copperplate engraving of the Death and Assumption of the Virgin (Plate 72). About actual size. · C. Saint Peter. Copperplate engraving. Executed by the Master of the Year 1446. Kaiser Friedrich Museum, Berlin. About actual size.

IV · COPPERPLATE ENGRAVINGS · 4, 5

74

The Virgin and Child Enthroned between Saint Theodore and Saint Catherine. Copperplate engraving. Designed and executed by Baldini about 1460–1463. Location unknown.
Reduced.

IV · COPPERPLATE ENGRAVINGS · 4, 5

A

B

A. The Agony in the Garden. Detail from a copperplate engraving. Executed by the Master of the Year 1446. Kaiser Friedrich Museum, Berlin. Enlarged. · B. The Agony in the Garden. Detail from a copperplate engraving. Designed and executed by Baldini about 1463–1464. Albertina, Vienna. About actual size.

IV · COPPERPLATE ENGRAVINGS · 4, 5

B

A

A. The Entombment. Copperplate engraving. Executed by the Master of the Year 1446. Kaiser Friedrich Museum, Berlin. Enlarged. · B. The Entombment. Copperplate engraving. Designed and executed by Baldini about 1463–1464. Albertina, Vienna. Reduced.

IV · COPPERPLATE ENGRAVINGS · 4, 5

B

A

A. Pietà. Copperplate engraving. Executed by the Master of the Year 1446. Kaiser Friedrich Museum, Berlin. Reproduced in reverse. Enlarged. · B. Pietà. Copperplate engraving. Designed and engraved by Baldini about 1463–1464. Albertina, Vienna. Reduced.

IV · COPPERPLATE ENGRAVINGS · 4, 5

78

B

A

A. Christ Carrying the Cross. Woodcut illustration
from the block book *Passion of Our Lord*. Printed
in Venice about 1450. Kaiser Friedrich Museum,

Berlin. · B. Christ Carrying the Cross. Copperplate
engraving. Designed and executed by Baldini about
1463–1464. Albertina, Vienna. Reduced.

IV · COPPERPLATE ENGRAVINGS · 4, 5

The Flagellation. Detail from a copperplate engraving. Designed and executed by Baldini about 1463–1464. Albertina, Vienna. About actual size.

IV · COPPERPLATE ENGRAVINGS · 4, 5

The Mass of Saint Gregory. Copperplate engraving. Executed by Baldini about 1463–1464. Seraglio Library, Istanbul. Reduced.

IV · COPPERPLATE ENGRAVINGS · 4, 5

The Mass of Saint Gregory. Copperplate engraving. Executed by the Master of the
Banderoles. British Museum, London. Reduced.

IV · COPPERPLATE ENGRAVINGS · 4, 5

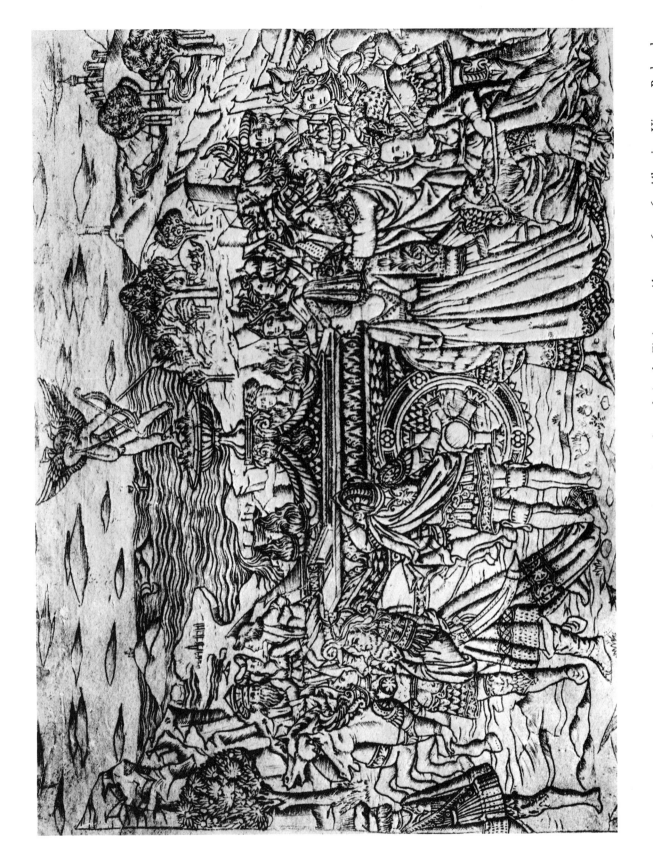

The Triumph of Love. Copperplate engraving. Executed by Baldini after a design by Finiguerra. About 1463–1464. Albertina, Vienna. Reduced.
IV · COPPERPLATE ENGRAVINGS · 4, 5

Three Humanists. Detail from the copperplate engraving of the Planet Jupiter. Executed
by Baldini after Finiguerra's engraving of the same subject, designed by Finiguerra in
collaboration with Pollaiuolo. About 1464–1465. British Museum, London. Enlarged.

IV · COPPERPLATE ENGRAVINGS · 4, 5

A

B

A. Head of a Young Man. Detail from a niello pax of the Crucifixion (Plate 33).
Engraved by Baldini as a variant of a pax engraved by Finiguerra. About 1464–
1465. · B. Head of Petrarch. Detail from the copperplate engraving of the Planet Jupiter
(see also Plate 83). Executed by Baldini after Finiguerra's engraving of the same subject,
designed by Finiguerra in collaboration with Pollaiuolo. About 1464–1465.

IV · COPPERPLATE ENGRAVINGS · 4, 5

Pilate Washing His Hands. Detail from the copperplate engraving of the Judgment
Hall of Pilate (Plate 106). Executed by Baldini after a design by Botticelli. About
1465–1475. Reduced.

IV · COPPERPLATE ENGRAVINGS · 4, 5

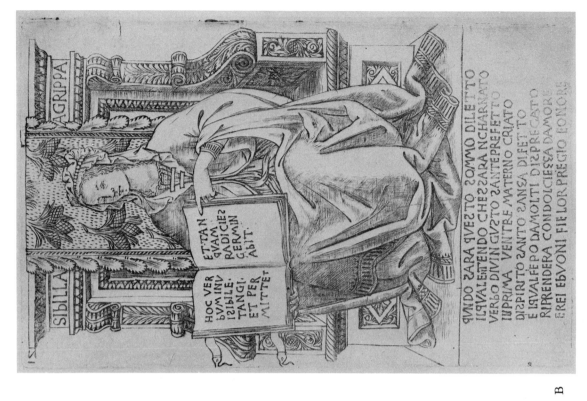

A. The Virgin and Child Standing before a Throne with Saint Sebastian and Saint Catherine. Copperplate engraving. Executed by Baldini after a design from the Finiguerra-Pollaiuolo workshop. About 1465–1475. Bibliothèque Nationale, Paris. Reduced. · B. The Sibyl Agrippa. Copperplate engraving. Executed by Baldini after a design from the Finiguerra-Pollaiuolo workshop. About 1465–1475. Bibliothèque Nationale, Paris. Reduced.

IV · COPPERPLATE ENGRAVINGS · 4, 5

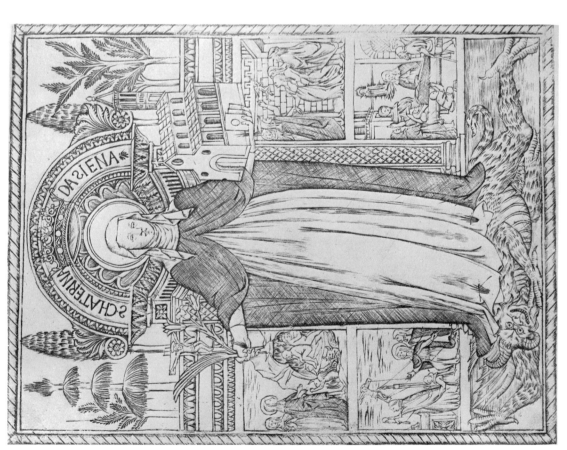

A. Saint Catherine of Siena. Copperplate engraving. Executed by Baldini after a design from the Finiguerra-Pollaiuolo workshop. About 1465–1475. British Museum, London. Reduced. · B. The Erythrean Sibyl. Copperplate engraving. Executed by Baldini after a design from the Finiguerra-Pollaiuolo workshop. About 1465–1475. British Museum, London. Reduced.

IV · COPPERPLATE ENGRAVINGS · 4, 5

God the Father. Bronze tabernacle door made by Ghiberti in 1450. Hospital of Santa Maria Nuova, Florence.

IV · COPPERPLATE ENGRAVINGS · 4, 5

Noah. Copperplate engraving. Executed by Baldini after a design from the Finiguerra-
Pollaiuolo workshop. About 1465–1475. Albertina, Vienna. Enlarged.
IV · COPPERPLATE ENGRAVINGS · 4, 5

Amazon. Detail from the Picture-Chronicle. Drawn by Finiguerra, probably in 1464.
British Museum, London. About actual size.

IV · COPPERPLATE ENGRAVINGS · 4, 5

Judith with the Head of Holophernes. Copperplate engraving. Executed by Baldini about
1465–1480, after a drawing in Finiguerra's Picture-Chronicle. Art Institute of Chicago.
Enlarged.

IV · COPPERPLATE ENGRAVINGS · 4, 5

Jason and Medea. Page from the Picture-Chronicle. Drawn by Finiguerra, probably in 1464. British Museum, London. Reduced.

IV · COPPERPLATE ENGRAVINGS · 4, 5

Jason and Medea. Copperplate engraving. Executed by Baldini about 1465–1480, after
a drawing in Finiguerra's Picture-Chronicle. British Museum, London. Enlarged.

IV · COPPERPLATE ENGRAVINGS · 4, 5

94

Noah. Detail from a bronze relief on Ghiberti's second Baptistry doors, which were set in place in 1452. Baptistry, Florence.

IV · COPPERPLATE ENGRAVINGS · 4, 5

Story of the Creation. Copperplate engraving. Executed by Baldini after a design from the Finiguerra-Pollaiuolo workshop. About 1465–1480. Albertina, Vienna. Reduced.

IV · COPPERPLATE ENGRAVINGS · 4, 5

Hell: the Torments of the Damned. Copperplate illustration from the *Monte Sancto di Dio* (1477). Executed by Baldini after a fresco attributed to Orcagna. British Museum, London. About actual size.

IV · COPPERPLATE ENGRAVINGS · 4, 5

opposite:
A. The City of Dis and the Punishments of Heresy. Copperplate illustration from Dante's *Divina Commedia* with a commentary by Landino (1481). Executed by Baldini after a design by Botticelli. British Museum, London. Reduced. · B. The City of Dis and the Punishments of Heresy. Drawn by Botticelli during the last quarter of the fifteenth century. Vatican Library, Rome.

A

B

IV · COPPERPLATE ENGRAVINGS · 4, 5

B

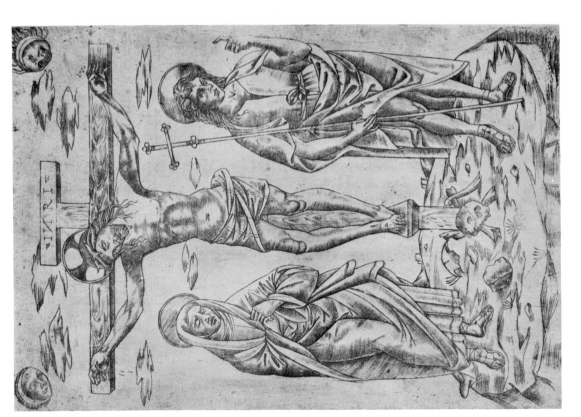

A

A. Christ on the Cross between the Virgin and Saint John. Copperplate engraving. Executed by Baldini about 1480–1487 (?). British Museum, London. Reduced. · B. Tobias and the Angel. Copperplate engraving. Executed by Baldini about 1480–1487 (?). Bibliothèque Nationale, Paris. Reduced.

IV · COPPERPLATE ENGRAVINGS · 4, 5

The Story of the Dead King and His Sons. Copperplate engraving. Executed by Baldini about 1480–1487 (?). British Museum, London. Reduced.

IV · COPPERPLATE ENGRAVINGS · 4, 5

The Adoration of the Magi. Detail from the copperplate engraving of the same subject. Executed by Rosselli after a design by Botticelli. About 1465–1475. British Museum, London. About actual size.

IV · COPPERPLATE ENGRAVINGS · 6

The Nativity. Copperplate engraving (from the series of the Life of the Virgin and of Christ). Executed by Rosselli after a design by Botticelli. About 1465–1475. British Museum, London. Reduced.

IV · COPPERPLATE ENGRAVINGS · 6

A

B

A. The Virgin, Saint John, and Soldiers. Detail from the copperplate engraving of Christ
Bearing the Cross (from the series of the Life of the Virgin and of Christ). Executed
by Rosselli after a design by Botticelli. About 1465–1475. British Museum, London.
About actual size. · B. Soldiers. Detail from the copperplate engraving of David and
Goliath. Executed by Rosselli after a design by Botticelli. About 1465–1475. Louvre
(Rothschild collection), Paris. Reduced.

IV · COPPERPLATE ENGRAVINGS · 6

B

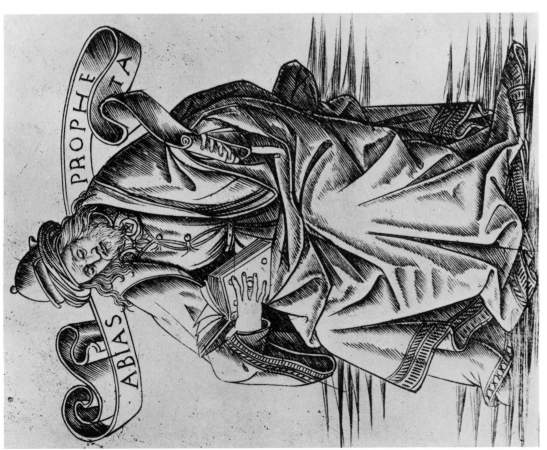

A

A. Obadiah. Detail from the copperplate engraving from the second series of the Prophets. Executed by Rosselli after a design by Botticelli. About 1465–1475. Metropolitan Museum, New York. Enlarged · B. Seated Figure. Detail from the copperplate engraving of Christ Disputing with the Doctors (from the series of the Life of the Virgin and of Christ). Executed by Rosselli after a design by Botticelli. About 1465–1475. British Museum, London. Enlarged.

IV · COPPERPLATE ENGRAVINGS · 6

A

B

A. Landscape. Detail from the copperplate engraving of the Assumption of the Virgin
(from the series of the Life of the Virgin and of Christ). Executed by Rosselli after a
design by Botticelli. About 1465–1475. British Museum, London. Enlarged. · B. Landscape. Detail from the copperplate engraving of the Triumph of Love (from the series
of the Triumphs of Petrarch). Executed by Rosselli after a design by Botticelli. About
1465–1475. British Museum, London. Enlarged.

IV · COPPERPLATE ENGRAVINGS · 6

B

A

A. Detail from the copperplate engraving of the Conversion of Paul. Executed by Baldini after a design by Botticelli.
About 1465–1475. Kunsthalle, Hamburg. Reduced · B. Detail from the copperplate engraving of David and Goliath.
Executed by Rosselli after a design by Botticelli. About 1465–1475. Louvre (Rothschild collection), Paris. Reduced.

IV · COPPERPLATE ENGRAVINGS · 6

The Judgment Hall of Pilate. Copperplate engraving. Executed by Baldini after a
design by Botticelli. About 1465–1475. Museum of Fine Arts, Boston. Reduced.

IV · COPPERPLATE ENGRAVINGS · 6

Solomon and the Queen of Sheba. Copperplate engraving. Executed by Rosselli after a design by Botticelli. About 1465–1475. British Museum, London. Reduced.

IV · COPPERPLATE ENGRAVINGS · 6

The Annunciation. Part of a composition painted by Fra Filippo Lippi about 1440. San Lorenzo, Florence.

IV · COPPERPLATE ENGRAVINGS · 6

opposite:
A. The Annunciation. Copperplate engraving (from the series of the Life of the Virgin and of Christ). Executed by Rosselli after a design by Botticelli. About 1465–1475. British Museum, London. Reduced. · B. The Annunciation. Painted by Botticelli in 1488. Uffizi, Florence.

A

B

IV · COPPERPLATE ENGRAVINGS · 6

A

B

A. Salome. Detail from the fresco of the Banquet of Herod. Painted by Fra Filippo Lippi in the early 1460s. Duomo, Prato. · B. Dancing Maiden. Detail from the copperplate engraving of the Triumph of Love (from the series of the Triumphs of Petrarch). Executed by Rosselli after a design by Botticelli. About 1465–1475. British Museum, London. Enlarged.

IV · COPPERPLATE ENGRAVINGS · 6

opposite:
A. The Presentation in the Temple. Fresco painted by Fra Filippo Lippi's follower Fra Diamante about 1468–1470. Prato Museum. · B. The Presentation in the Temple. Detail from a copperplate engraving (from the series of the Life of the Virgin and of Christ). Executed by Rosselli after a design by Botticelli. About 1465–1475. British Museum, London. About actual size.

A

B

112

A

B

A. Landscape. Detail from the copperplate engraving of a view of Florence. Designed and executed by Rosselli after 1480. Società Colombaria, Florence. Enlarged. · B. Landscape. Detail from the copperplate engraving of the Triumph of Love (from the series of the Triumphs of Petrarch). Executed by Rosselli after a design by Botticelli. About 1465–1475. British Museum, London. Enlarged.

IV · COPPERPLATE ENGRAVINGS · 6